PAULENE

My Extraordinary Kiwi Mate
Some Stories of Our Life Together

Harry Foster

Copyright © 2023
All Rights Reserved

These stories are about some of the adventures we had together. We were together for 57 years and were due to have our 55th wedding anniversary just three weeks after she passed away on June 7, 2022.

Table of Contents

Dedication v

Acknowledgements ii

About the Author iii

Chapter One 1
    How and where we met, and our hitchhiking trip to Darwin..

Chapter Two 26
    Our stay in Darwin, working, and forging our relationship..

Chapter Three 36
    Our hitchhiking trip from Darwin to Alice, south, then across the Nullarbor to Perth ....

Chapter Four 60
    Our seven-week bicycle trip from Ottawa to Mexico in 1970..

Chapter Five 146
    Our seven-week 820-mile canoe trip from Sault St. Marie to Ottawa, Ontario ....

Chapter Six 202
    Lake Superior North Shore by canoe, Cloud Bay to Marathon August 1980 ....

Chapter Seven 229
    Lake Superior North Shore, Marathon to Michipicoten August 1976...............................

Chapter Eight 253
    Lake Superior North Shore, Michipicoten to Sault St Marie, July 1979..........................

Chapter Nine 270
    Our fifth French River Long Weekend trip, June 1980..

Epilogue 303

Dedication

This book is dedicated to the memory of my wife and best friend Paulene, and for her many New Zealand, Canadian and American, family and friends.

Acknowledgements

I first have to acknowledge Paulene my wife who passed away this past June 7, 2022. She instilled in me a love of learning through reading that has lasted a lifetime. This pretty well started in Darwin Australia where we stayed and worked for 6 months while saving for our ship passage from Perth Australia to Naples Italy. This was a period of intellectual growth for us both, as well as forging a relationship that would last for 57 years.

I also want to acknowledge the team at Amazon Publishing for their support and guidance in seeing this first project through. And thanks to all the friends, neighbours and family who encouraged me to do this book.

About the Author

This is Harry Foster's first book, but thinks there will be two more coming. In the early years Harry worked at a number of Jobs, starting off as an Office boy in an Advertising company, to aircraft maintenance to becoming a fitter-welder in Toronto. These skills served him well as he worked his way around the world after having met his future bride in Australia. His love of photography started in Singapore where he bought his first decent camera. After returning to Canada he went back to school to get his high school diploma, meanwhile developing his photography skills. He started work in the National Museums of Canada in 1969.

After 1.5 years, he and his wife decided to go back to New Zealand as Harry had not yet met his wife's family. They stayed almost 4 years before returning to Canada and Harry getting his Museum job back. During the years in New Zealand he worked with the Department of Scientific and Industrial Research as a photographer, picking up a lot of new skills. He worked with the Museums in Ottawa for 32 years before retiring in 2005.

Chapter One

How and where we met, and our hitchhiking trip to Darwin

The year was December 1965 when I went on to Australia after spending six months working and travelling in New Zealand.

My stay in New Zealand was a great highlight and a fortuitous place to start the adventure. The hospitality of the New Zealanders is something that has to be experienced to be believed. It is also a country of unequalled natural beauty. I soon got a job in a Hydraulics company in Auckland as a Fitter and Welder and stayed happily working there for my time in New Zealand.

It was one evening in New Zealand while talking to some newly acquired friends (this happens all the time) that I mentioned I might be soon moving on to Australia. One of them mentioned that if I was going to be staying in Sydney for any length of time, I must go and stay at a place called Rotorua House in Bondi Junction (a suburb).

He said it was a sort of boarding come guest house with mixed accommodation (men and women) run by a young New Zealand couple. Most of the inhabitants were young and travelling. Naturally, I filed this information away in the back of my mind.

As it happened, it was only a couple of weeks after this that I decided to move on, New Year's Day, as a matter of fact. As I still had my ticket to Sydney that I had bought in Canada, I just had to make the necessary reservations and hop on the jet. I arrived in Sydney at 11 am. January 1, 1966. While coming in for a landing after flying over the Tasman Sea, I was looking down at the coastline with its many beaches and then at Sydney itself. I had an overwhelming feeling come over me that I would enjoy Sydney and Australia very, very much. I then took a bus into downtown Sydney and left my bags with the Qantas Airlines people, grabbed a cab and headed for Bondi Junction.

When we arrived, I asked the driver if he happened to know where this Rotorua House might be. He didn't. I then got out and wandered around and asked a few more people without success. Naturally, I was feeling a little sad that I couldn't find this place. I sat down and thought, well, I'll need accommodation anyway and if I can find some here, all the better, as it is near the world-renowned Bondi Beach.

Through a newspaper, it wasn't long before I found a room in another boarding house. Even though it wasn't exactly what I wanted, it would suffice until I got my bearings.

I was only there two days when while walking down to Bondi Beach, I struck up a conversation with a girl also walking towards the beach, and would you believe, she had a number of friends who lived at Rotorua House. Needless to say, I went straight over in the morning, had a talk with the landlady and moved in that afternoon.

This was, without a doubt, one of the most interesting places in which I have lived. There were 32 of us, and all were in the age group of 20-29 years. There were people from all four corners of the globe, and a most interesting bunch, as we were all in various stages of travel. There were very few places in the world where one of us had not been. This was where I met the other three individuals that would make up the hitchhiking party to Darwin.

Paulene Sinclair: A very special girl from Hastings, New Zealand and my future bride.

Norm Campbell: From Ottawa, Canada, who, like me, was on a working holiday in this part of the world.

Jodie Bothwell: Norm's girlfriend who hails from the City of Perth in West Australia.

The way I actually met Paulene was funny, too, as we were sitting on the floor in the TV room of the boarding house one evening when Paulene pulled out a cigarette. Me being the gentleman that I am, I reached over to light it and not only lit the cigarette but her lovely blond hair too. Quick pat pat pat pat to put it out, and one could say that was the start of the romance which continues to this day.

We all held jobs in Sydney, but there were many days off called 'Sickie's' for trips to the beaches and surrounding country. In short, we had a ball.

Sydney is one of the most alive towns I've had the pleasure of living in. If we had a day where a gang of us planned to go to one of the beaches or the mountains for an outing, one of the girls in the boarding house would go around with pad and paper, get people's boss' phone numbers and the excuse why that particular person would sadly not be able to make it in today.

It was actually two weeks before our date of departure that we decided to go to Darwin. Naturally, we were all interested in seeing more of Australia, but one of the main reasons that prompted our leaving Sydney was, in effect, money.

As long as we stayed in a town like Sydney, we would save little or none of the money that we earned. As much as we all loved the atmosphere and the fun to be had, it would put a damper on our future plans for travel.

We chose Darwin as it is high up in the tropics where none of us had ever lived or worked before, and the fact that the wages are the highest of anywhere in Australia would be a new and very interesting experience, to say the least. The wages in Darwin are higher because it is so far isolated from the rest of Australia and for the fact of its severe climate.

It seemed like years for those two weeks to pass. But pass they did, and on the final day, our excitement was beyond description. There was a farewell party for us the night before, and what a party that was.

The next morning we were all up early. Who could sleep with a 3200-mile hitchhiking trip ahead of them? We still had to put in most of the day as our first ride, which was prearranged with one of the fellows living at Rotorua House, wasn't going to start until 5.30 pm. Norm and I went down to Bondi beach to get a couple of souvenir photographs. This was quite amusing as it was a dull and chilly day, and when we arrived at the beach, there were only about five people on it. Never had we seen it so deserted, (this is what it normally looks like on a good day).

After lunch, the four of us took in a movie, and before we knew it, the time had gone, and it was time to go.

The farewell in front of Rotorua House was very sad, and a few tears were shed. Doug Sheridan was heading north to Port Macquarie for a holiday and offered to give us a lift as far as he went, which was about 260 miles up the coast and a very big help.

Being all packed, we had just to put our gear in Doug's car, a Holden Utility. This vehicle could only seat three inside, so two would ride out back in the tray. Norman and Jodie started off in the back, then after a little over 100 miles Paulene and I got in the back for a spell so Jodie and Norm could warm up. When we left Rotorua House, Norman and I converted a bed mattress to put in the back of the truck. With this, a blanket and a tarpaulin, we could get very comfortable.

The trip itself to where Doug left us was uneventful except for many laughs. The place was called Oxford Highway Junction, and we arrived at about 1.30 am

After the goodbyes, there we were, right in the middle of nowhere. We had thought we would shoot right through, but as it happened, there was very little traffic... like none. After about an hour and a half with no cars going by, we decided to try and get some sleep. We had taken the mattress out of the truck with the rest of our gear, and we put it at the side of the road, and the four of us promptly collapsed on it.

We slept off and on sporadically until 5 am. There were many laughs as we must have been quite a sight as there we were just 8" off the highway, trucks and cars zooming close by. With all the deadly snakes in Australia, there was no way we were going to go into a field and lie down. We awoke looking a little dishevelled but soon rectified that by using the water from our canteens for washing etc.

After tidying up a bit and disposing of the mattress, we were raring to go and expecting a ride that would take us right to Darwin Ha Ha. Two hours later, a fellow in a beat-up old truck stopped and gave us a lift three miles up the road and put us out, again right in the middle of nowhere, but the scenery was different anyway.

By this time, we were beginning to get a bit peckish, and as there was a cornfield across the road, we helped ourselves to a few ears. With a bit of imagination, raw corn can be quite nice, you know. Not to worry, fifteen minutes later, a fellow in a bread truck stopped and gave us a loaf of bread. He was an awfully nice and interesting person who stayed and talked for a few minutes. I asked him if he would break bread with us, but he said as he had more deliveries to make, he had better be on his way. He was the first of many fabulous people we were going to encounter on our trip.

After a further wait of an hour and a half without getting a ride, we decided something had to be done. We figured that if we split up, our chances of getting a lift would be greatly improved.

Paulene and I hoisted our bags onto our heads and staggered down the road about a mile. Within a short while, two boys picked us up and took us through to Kempsey, where we had a wash and something to eat.

Our next ride was with a chap travelling north about 100 miles. He also had another hitchhiker in the car, a Kiwi heading for Cairns. Half way, the car had a puncture, but otherwise, the trip was uneventful.

Harry thumbing a ride in the hot sun with our Darwin sign. Crazy looking back, suitcases instead of backpacks which we would later use. Also, notice my footwear... plastic flip-flops

Thumbing once again, and this time very successfully, as the man who stopped was going to Brisbane, although we had arranged to meet Norman and Jodie at Coolangatta, which is about 50 miles south of Brisbane. He had a Utility with two beautiful Boxer dogs on the back. Very interesting guy as he had done a lot of travelling around Queensland and the Northern Territory.

We arrived at Coolangatta at about 7.30 pm - we were now at the New South Wales/Queensland border. Luckily we met up with Norman and Jodie within a short while, so after a clean-up and a meal, we deposited ourselves on the beach for the night. We were already noticing the change in the temperature.

Woke around 6 am, and while Jodie and Norman had a swim and Paulene slept in, I went for a walk around Coolangatta to find a Laundrette where we could have a shower.

On the road at the disgraceful hour of 10.15 am and then a long wait in the heat. Our first ride was with a fellow who had lived up in Darwin and the Territories for many years. It wasn't really a ride, but he saw our sign, "Darwin", so he picked us up and took us to the other side of town and showed us around, plus giving us all kinds of information and addresses in Darwin. If all the people up there are like him, then it should be fabulous.

We were then picked up by a young boy going to Brisbane, which was a large, sprawling city, which we found most uninteresting. We couldn't wait to get back out to the bush.

On the outskirts of Brisbane, we were picked up by a guy in another Holden Utility. We passed Norman and Jodie a little further down the highway, so he stopped, and they piled on the back. He took us to a small country town Caboolture, where the four of us split up again, Paulene and I getting a ride on a truck to Nambour, which was a really beautiful little town in the heart of the pineapple and banana plantations. Our next ride was very slow, but he was a nice old man, and he took us through to Bundaberg, arriving about 9 pm. As we were still reasonably fresh, we decided to keep hitching through the night if there were any rides.

Out of the darkness, a funny-looking chap appeared, a little under the weather. He told us we were standing in the wrong place to get a ride and so helped us with our bags around the corner and along a road to a much better position. After saying goodbye, we were just deciding which would be the best tree to sleep under as there were no cars, who should arrive back but him, inviting us to his place for coffee. Not knowing what to expect, we accepted. We met his mother and his dying grandmother, who were very kind to us, giving us a lovely meal of cold meat and vegetables, and insisting we stay the night. After a good breakfast, we set off the next morning at about 7.30 am feeling very refreshed. We were certainly very grateful to Terry and his mother.

The house in the middle is where they lived

The first car that came along stopped; it certainly seemed our lucky day. It was driven by a Commercial Traveller who took us to the bypass, which was about 13 miles out of Gladstone.

The traveller gave us an address of an Engineer in Darwin and also the address of a friend of his in Hobart, Tasmania. Well, we only waited for 15 minutes at the Gladstone bypass when we got a ride with a Traveller going through to Rockhampton. Ten miles south of Rockhampton, we passed the Tropic of Capricorn. Got out in Rockhampton and were walking through town when a woman stopped and gave us a lift to the outskirts, where we just happened to meet Norman and Jodie.

We jumped up and down, and there was much excitement and lots to tell each other about our experiences in the last 24 hours. Jodie and Norman had been in Rockhampton standing in the sun since 10 am; it was 12 noon when we met them.

We then split up and tried to get lifts again. We all stood out in the sun till 2.00 pm. It was 105°, and so on the verge of total collapse, we decided to find a pub and have a drink and a feed.

At 5.00 pm, we split up again. Fifteen minutes later, a car stopped for Norman and Jodie, and they called us to come. Ten minutes later, we were all off to Townsville, 516 miles away, time 5.30 pm on Feb. 15/1966.

We stopped alongside the highway in the middle of the night for 4 hours. Paulene and I put a rug on the roof of the car, covered ourselves with mosquito netting and had a good sleep (or at least I did).

This little experience has never left me, as at no time before or since have we ever witnessed the night sky so alive with stars and planets we felt we could reach up and touch them. This must have been the best Dark Sky situation. We passed through some real outback country; one place, there was a stretch of 200 miles with nothing in between except one service station at the halfway point.

The fellows we rode with were George, who was 17 and apparently had run away from home in Sydney. The driver and owner of the car (Austin Westminster) was Jim, 18 years old but quite a nice and very sensible sort of guy. We arrived in Townsville at 11.45 a. m. Feb. 16/66 after being in the car for 18 hours.

When we arrived at Townsville, the first thing to do was find a motel with a swimming pool where we could get a good rest for our long trip ahead. This was our halfway point, and we wanted to treat ourselves. We found a nice motel called the Coolabah, with a marvellous pool, banana trees, and pleasant rooms.

The motel we stayed in at Townsville was the Coolabah and is still there but has lost a lot of its charm and is now on a four-lane roadway. I am sure the banana trees and perhaps the pool are long gone too.

We booked in and were shown to our rooms. George came and saw our rooms, then he and Jim just disappeared, and Paulene saw them drive away. We had not even said goodbye to them. Anyway, we sort of put them out of our minds and thought oh well, I guess we won't see them again. So we all had a shower, and a swim in the pool, then flopped down for a rest. I had my wallet beside me on the dressing table, and Norman had his beside him on his bed. After a couple of hours of sleep, Norman was woken up by these two guys who came into our room. I was still asleep, and the fellows spoke to Norman and asked if they could come back in an hour and watch T.V. Norman said okay, as they had given us a lift for more than 500 miles, so that was the least we could do.

Norman got up 10 minutes later and went to iron a shirt; I was still asleep. Now in this interval of 6 minutes, while Norman was gone and I was asleep, George and Jim must have returned and stolen both Norman and my wallets. Norman's containing all his papers plus £3 (he keeps his money elsewhere) and my wallet, which to me was priceless, and £21 (two-thirds of my money).

We talked it over for a while amongst ourselves and decided it had to be them, so we called the police, and they sent a detective around. Sgt. Det. Watson. He was a nice sort of bloke, and we gave him a most detailed description of the car and the boys and their names. I also told him of the Deputy Sheriff's badge I had in my wallet that was stolen too.

I was given that badge when a friend and I had hitchhiked around the US when we were 16. We spent three weeks in San Antonio with friends of my buddy's family, and while there helped him in his Hay Bailing job. When we left San Antonio and continued west, I was given this badge as a memento of our stay there. We were told by the police that they were looking for these two lads in connection with a job in Southport. In all probability, our ride of 560 miles to Townsville had been in a stolen car. We kind of moped around for a while, feeling sorry for our misfortune, but then realized there was nothing we could do about it, so we went about really enjoying our stay at the Coolabah with lots of swimming and plenty of good food. A photo of Paulene, Norman and Jodi beside the pool and one of Paulene with a bunch of bananas growing right there at the motel. They did not even taste like the bananas we are familiar with, rather like a fruit salad taste. Awesome!

Thursday morning, after a huge breakfast of steak and eggs and a swim, we packed up and left. The four of us got a cab to the outskirts of town. It was very hot, about 95° and with high humidity. We tossed a coin for the best position on the highway, and Paulene and I won. We only had to wait about half an hour and then got a lift to Charters Towers 80 miles away, arriving at 1.30 pm.

He left us in the middle of town, not on the main road. I didn't like the look of the position from a hitch-hiking standpoint, but we stayed for a couple of hours without one single car going through. At this time, a couple of old men came along to talk to us. They were sun-wrinkled old men with cloudy, far-away-looking eyes but very pleasant. One of them talked to Paulene for about 10 minutes before remarking oh, you're a lady; he thought he was talking to a couple of lads.

Then a little boy came along and asked us if we wanted a drink of water. Paulene and I went over to his house and met his mum, who was very nice and very hospitable. We had a drink of cordial and a very interesting talk with her as she and her husband had lived all over the territory. It then started to rain, so we brought our bags over and put them into the garage.

After the rain, we thought we would walk around and have a look at the town and maybe find a better position to get a lift. Charters Towers had been a boom town in the gold rush days and had 70 pubs (a lot of them still standing). It was still the same; nothing seemed to have changed or modernized; it looked as if it had come right out of the wild west.

This hotel was one that was saved, restored and turned into the town library.

We walked towards the outskirts of town, and as we came around a corner, who should we meet but Norman and Jodie so there was much rejoicing. Paulene and I then walked back and got our bags. A few minutes after we returned, Norman and Jodie got a ride to Pentland and shortly after, a small land-rover stopped for us and told us he was going through to Mt. Isa. It was full of his gear, so Paulene rode in

the front, and I piled in the back. This was 5.30 pm Thursday. We got as far as Pentland, whereby some good luck. I saw Norman on the front porch of the pub. We stopped, and I ran back to speak to them. Norman came back to the land rover with me, and within 10 minutes, we were all piled in the rover heading for Mt. Isa.

That night we got as far as Hughenden. We slept in the Land-Rover a couple of miles outside of town which wasn't very comfortable either. Slowly waking up after an uncomfortable night crammed into the small Land-Rover. 5 of us. Notice all the flies on Norman's back and the cover of the Land Rover. The telling of the flies of the Australian Outback is one thing, but one really has to experience it to believe it.

The fellow we were riding with owns and services a fleet of jute boxes throughout Queensland and the Northern Territory, so in Hughenden, he had three machines to attend to. One was a pub and the other a restaurant, both in the middle of nowhere. How these people could live in those conditions, I will never know. The bugs (all shapes and sizes) and flies were just unbelievable and the filth. After a few hours at Hughenden, we pushed on to Richmond, as he had a few machines there to attend to. Richmond had quite a nice swimming pool, so after a shower, we all retired to the pool for a couple of hours. After a feed, we pushed on to Julia Creek.

This is what so many roads looked like as you navigated the outback. One did not often wonder what was around the next corner.

The road or track was two marks of tyres and grass growing in the middle. We bounced around the land rover for 100 miles. Our backs were all sore, and my flight bag got battered and ripped. The road was also washed out in quite a few places, and it was just as well we were in a land rover, or we wouldn't have gotten through. This spot has been washed out and rebuilt so many times.

We arrived at Julia Creek at about 12.45 pm. It had been a hell of a trip from Richmond, and we were all very hot and dry, so the first thing we did was have a beer. Steve had five machines at Julia, so we dived into the swimming pool for a couple of hours.

We left Julia Creek at 4.45 pm and had a good trip through to Mt. Isa with bitumen road all the way. The scenery was different, more mountainous with millions of ant hills, some 6-7 ft tall and 3-4 ft thick. Also saw skeletons of dead cattle on the side of the road that had died from the heat.

We arrived at Mt. Isa at 7.15, and after Steve drove us around for a while, we thought it better to book into a hotel rather than sleep on the side of the road. This we did at the Boyd Hotel; it looked like it was plucked straight out of a wild west movie. Cost £2.10s each.

This is the Boyd Hotel that we stayed at one night. Loved those Aussi hotels with the wrap-around verandas to help control the heat.

We had a walk around town and spoke to the police about the Townsville incident. Lots of pubs and people, mostly guys, everywhere. All kinds of noise and song flowed out of the pub windows and doors, guys staggering along the streets and even an odd one sleeping on the sidewalk. A very wild and woolly frontier town. We all had a good night's sleep at the hotel and under mosquito netting, which was a real treat.

We woke at about 8 am, got cleaned up and were on the road again by 9.15. We split up again about 1 mile apart. Paulene and I stood there for about 2 hours; a few people stopped but were only going as far as the local lake. Then this cute redhead came along on a motor scooter, not wearing very much considering the sun. We talked for a while; then, she invited us back to her flat for lunch. The problem was our baggage, so off she went to the Barkley, the poshest hotel motel in town and came back with the manager who transported our luggage back to her flat. Jo was a fabulous type with a tremendous personality and also supplied us with a delicious lunch and watermelon. We were introduced to her flatmate (well-travelled who gave me addresses in Europe), and then Rachael and her boyfriend drove us out to the outskirts of town to a good position at a Rodeo ground.

We were at the Rodeo Ground for about two hours when Jodie and Norman came along. They had had a rough afternoon and were very hot and tired. Together we waited about 1/2 an hour when three came along in a Utility, so we all piled on the back, and they gave us a lift 120 miles to a place called Camooweal, arriving at approximately 8.30 pm.

The town consisted of two pubs, two cafes and a few assorted shacks, plus about 14 zillion bugs of all shapes and sizes. Sleeping out as we had intended doing was out of the question, so we got a room for 10-bob each (after a bit of bickering) in a ghastly old pub.

This was our 10-bob accommodation at Camooweal, and we didn't even have to pay extra for the bugs. The red arrow points to our spot for the night. Historic photo.

Above is what that old place looks like today. It also serves as the Barkley Tableland Heritage Centre

Well, what a room - the skungy old beds were about 2 feet wide. Walking across the room, your feet would not actually touch wood; one was walking only on bugs. There were more bugs in there than in the whole of Canada. I had a 9 ft mosquito net, so I managed to keep a few bugs off Paulene and I, but poor Norman and Jodie were eaten alive. It was a hell of a night, the humidity was in the thousands, and even though I had the net, the bugs still had a feed.

Lazed around until noon of the next day until we were put out of our room. There was absolutely no traffic whatsoever in either direction. The flies were out in force, and the temperature was over 100°. Paulene and I sat on the verandah of the hotel with a mosquito netting over us, which made quite a picture (I wish I had one).

Norman and Jodie bought little mosquito nets to fit on their hats and cover their faces. Looked like a couple of beekeepers. Shortly after, we invested in some; they were the greatest invention in the world.

4 pm came along, and we figured we would be there for a few days, dead, or worse, because only five vehicles had passed in all that time, and for various reasons, they couldn't take us. Then I saw this big truck rambling into town, and he pulled over a ways up the road. I went up and asked him where he was going, and he said 'Darwin'. I asked him if we could hop aboard, and he said sure, but it won't be comfortable. I told we had roughed it before, so we climbed on.

It was a big trailer with three horses, horse feed and petrol. We sort of made ourselves comfortable on the bags of chaff, and this is how we stayed for two nights and two days.

The truck was driven by the owner of a big station (ranch) near Adelaide River. With him was a new man he had hired to boss the Jackaroos (cowboys) at his station. Behind the truck followed his wife and two young boys in a Holden Station wagon towing a caravan.

They were very interesting people and told us all about station life and life in general in the territory. Our meals consisted of canned meat (stews etc.), fruit, and bread. One time we even filled our canteens with water from a puddle.

The countryside was absolutely flat, and the road was as straight as an arrow for long distances. We joined the Stuart Highway at a place called Three Ways. I wish I had taken a picture here, but perhaps I was out of film. The photo would have been of an older aboriginal man sitting cross-legged on the grass, cutting it with a pair of scissors. Heading north now, when we reached Katherine, we started to climb, and we noticed the difference in the vegetation, as it was changing to more tropical-type trees.

The truck let us off at Adelaide River, and we immediately had a ride straight through to Darwin. We arrived in Darwin at 5.30 pm. on Wednesday, 23rd February, and as we got out of our last car, it poured with rain, and I'm sure we looked like a very bedraggled crew, but… we were in Darwin.

We went straight to the welfare office, and I said to the fellow behind the counter, 'We need help' He laughed and said, 'get outta here' go and see what you can do before coming back here. We finally went to a boarding house, and they gave us three days' lodging, with my funny old camera as security.

Paulene and I got jobs the next day; hers was at the welfare office, turns out they had an ad in the local paper looking for the skills that Paulene had. I got a job as a Welder-fitter in a shop where I was the only non-Italian.

We both stayed in these jobs for the 5+ months we were in Darwin… saving all our money for the trip by sea, from Perth to Italy, that we planned while in Darwin.

Norm and Jodie decided not to stay in Darwin and headed back down south after a week or so. Norm came back to Ottawa eventually, and I made contact once when we finally got back here, but that never kept up. Would love to know what happened to Jodie, though, as we both really liked her.

Chapter Two

Our stay in Darwin, working, and forging our relationship

Our stay in Darwin, from Feb 23 to July 20, 1966, working, forging our relationship, and saving our money for what lay ahead.

Paulene moved into a girls' hostel, and I stayed at the boarding house. Paulene joked that her Grandmothers 'would be shocked' if they found out we were living together and not married.

Our life here was one of work, walking when not too hot; it didn't matter as long as we were together. Darwin in those days looked a lot different than it does now, as the old Darwin almost got blown away with Cyclone Tracy in 1974. Here are a few photos from when we were there.

The first one is of the Don Hotel. There was a small Chinese restaurant at the far right of the building, if I remember correctly. We could get a cheap feed of chicken fried rice or some other combination. As you can imagine, the Don Bamboo Lounge was a busy place in the evenings. We did not partake as we were saving all the money we could.

The next shot is one of the hostel that Paulene moved into from the boarding house. I was to move in there, too, after some time, which was much more convenient for us both.

The rooms were pretty small but comfortable. No glass in the windows, just slats that one could open and close. Even though we slept under mosquito netting, they were not a real bother; it was some of the other creatures that one wanted to keep away in order to get a good night's sleep. Here is Paulene in her room.

We joined the library and did some serious reading while in Darwin. Getting to know and appreciate some authors like Ralph Waldo Emerson, Montaigne, Lin

Yutang, Henry Miller, Emily Carr, Dostoevsky, John Paul Jones, Thoreau, Bernard Moitessier, John Steinbeck, and Robert Ardrey. This was a period of intellectual growth for us both as well as making our relationship stronger and stronger. Sometimes on walking from the hostel to the library in the early evening, we would see some Fox Bats hanging from the telephone wires. This was quite a site as they were huge, with a head not too unlike that of a fox, big teeth too. On the way home after our visit to the library, we sometimes saw them flying. They can have a 1.5-meter wingspan. For Paulene and me who only knew bats that could fit in your hand, this was amazing and a bit scary.

Here are a couple of photos of what the Darwin docks looked like in 1966.

This is a photo Paulene took of me walking along the beach near Darwin. Sometimes we would see family groups of Aborigines along remote beaches too, the men carrying long spears, I suppose they used for fishing.

Speaking of beaches. On extremely hot and humid days it was all you could do to walk a couple of kilometres. We had a beach we could walk to and felt it was our beach, quite secluded and private. In the wet season, you were not supposed to swim in the ocean because of the danger of getting stung by a sea wasp (box Jellyfish).

One article says the sea wasp is a (box jellyfish) with extremely potent and painful venom that has been known, in extreme cases, to kill people in as few as three minutes. The sea wasp's small body is less of a concern than the tentacles, which reach up to 10 feet (3 m) long. We were told by locals that they were most dangerous to older folk with heart conditions, but to be very watchful for them and don't go in deeper water as you do not want to get stung by one

We could not keep out of the water on days like this but were very watchful and we never got stung.

The other feature of this beach area that at first was shocking to us was our first encounter with a Sand Monitor (a type of lizard), or what is sometimes called the Racehorse Goanna for its speed, sometimes reaching 40kph. An average length of one can be 140 cm (4.6 ft) and weigh as much as 6 kg (13 lbs).

We were lying sunbathing on the hot sand with small bushes scattered here and there when we heard a noise behind us and on looking saw one of these creatures. It took off like a rocket making a lot of noise with its feet in the sand. Our eyes popped right out. Someone later told us if they appear to be running towards you, it might think you are a tree as they will climb these on occasion. If this happens, we were told the best thing to do is to lie down, so they don't think you are a tree. I'm sure glad we did not have to test that advice.

Paulene relaxing during a picnic near a beach outside of Darwin.

There was a fresh water swimming hole not too far from town that people would flock to on really hot days in order to not be tempted to swim in the Ocean and the risk of getting stung by a Sea Wasp.

Paulene worked for the Welfare office as a secretary while in Darwin, and I got a job as a Welder-fitter in a shop where I was the only non-Italian. It wasn't too long before I was speaking broken English, just like they did. They were a great bunch of guys. At this shop, we would fabricate whatever was asked of us. Bull bars were a common project for cars and trucks to protect them in case of hitting animals. I was also called on to do repair work at a local fuel depot and fit new and better baffles inside large tanker trucks that would deliver fuel through the outback.

The boss often lent me an open-style army jeep to go and meet Paulene at lunchtime for a break. She looked like she came off the pages of a fashion magazine and me in my sweat and dirt-stained coveralls. We never forgot the time we were enjoying a pub lunch when these mostly huge white men came in with very, very white skin. What a contrast to the burnt brown wrinkled skin of the locals. Turns out these were the British Lions Rugby club, who had some time to kill before their plane took them down south.

By July of 1966, we had saved up enough money to pay for two tickets that would take us by ship from Perth, Australia, to Naples in Italy. The next chapter details that hitchhiking trip from Darwin to Perth.

Chapter Three

Our hitchhiking trip from Darwin to Alice, south, then across the Nullarbor to Perth

Our hitchhiking trip from Darwin down through the middle of Australia, then across the Nullarbor plain to Perth on the west coast.

The day is Wednesday, the 20th of July 1966, and the start of our trip from Darwin to Perth, 2400 miles away. At 1 pm we called a taxi and took it to the outskirts of town near the airport. We only had to stand there for an hour, and in that time, we made a sign with Perth on it. A few cars stopped and offered us lifts, but they were only going a few miles down the track.

Then a white Holden station wagon happened along, and he stopped, but he was so full of suit cases and boxes it didn't look like he could fit one person in, let along the both of us and our gear. But he said let's give it a try. We took about 25 minutes rearranging his car, and we finally managed to fit everything in. We climbed in and introduced ourselves to each other. This fellow called George was a traveller (salesman) about 25 years old of east European decent and turned out to be a most interesting fellow. His line of good were ladies' sportswear and dolls etc.

His home base is in Brisbane, and his territory is all of Queensland and the Northern Territories, going right up the coast from Brisbane to Cairns, across to Mt Isa, then west and north to Darwin, and as far south as Alice Springs, plus all the real outback country of Queensland.

Regarding our ride with him, it would be south to Three Ways, a distance of 625 miles from Darwin and a great start to our trip. On the way south, we went in and saw the war Memorial and cemetery, which was very beautiful, being in a Jungle atmosphere with lots of gaily coloured birds about.

Further south, we stopped and took a few pictures beside a termite mound that was close to 20 ft high.

Travelling along the road, we saw many dead Kangaroos, a couple of wild pigs, and a dingo.

We arrived at Katherine at about 5:30, so we picked up a few groceries to eat in the car, then pressed on. We had a lot of fun with George, and in a couple of hours, it seemed like he was an old friend, not someone we had just met. We got to about 30 miles of Three Ways early in the morning and decided to sleep. George got his lie-low out and a few blankets, and he slept outside while Paulene and I slept in the front seat, and sleep we did for about 4 hours. Even with this little difference south, we noticed the change in climate as it was quite cool sleeping.

July 21, 1966

We rose with the sun and, in short order, were on our way again. We arrived at Three Ways at about 6:45 am. Three Ways is just a little road house at the junction of these roads going North, South, and East. There was not a sign of life when we arrived, but the washrooms were open, so we were able to have a good wash. At about 8 am, a fellow got up and went out back to start the motor that powered his generator. A few minutes later, George was able to get his car filled up with fuel, and then we bid each other adieu as he headed east towards Mount Isa while we were headed south towards Alice Springs.

Paulene and I then went in and had a nice big breakfast and a pot of coffee. We then positioned ourselves on the highway. It was a beautiful morning, clear, cool, and not a cloud in the sky. There was hardly any traffic at all on the road, so I was able to wander up the road a few hundred yards and talk to the other fellow who was hitchhiking to Darwin. He was a Kiwi bloke about my age who was working his way to India, where he was going to study Yoga. Quite an interesting fellow to talk to. I then saw a car in the distance, so I ran back to where Paulene was waiting.

As the car approached, I held out our sign, and he stopped. He was only going as far as Tennent Creek, 16 miles south, but we decided to take the lift as there might be traffic heading south from there. This fellow was a middle age guy and a very cheerful sort. His home was in New South Wales, but he was up here doing some oil exploration work. Very kindly, he drove us through town and let us out on the outskirts. So, here we were at Tennent Creek, and what a horrible dusty little place it is. The only reason it is here is because of its gold mine and a few other minerals. The surrounding country is very flat dry, and dusty. There are very few trees around, and if some of the buildings are painted a different colour from each other, it is hidden by the thick layer of dust that covers everything. We had horrible visions of being stuck here for a couple of days, but we only stood there for about 1/2 hour when we saw a big transport coming into and through town.

We flashed our sign, and much to our surprise, he stopped. I asked him if he was going as far as Alice Springs, and he said there was nowhere else to go. So I tied our packs on the back, and we piled in. The driver was a Kiwi bloke about 27 years old and seemed a nice lad. He had been in Australia for two years and had been driving the Territory for nine months.

Now, this truck he was driving was, to say the least, very interesting. It was a big Fodex diesel, and behind the cab were three huge trailers with 53 tons of native copper from the Pekoke mines worth $30,000. These large trucks were sometimes called Truck Trains, as some had up to 5 trailers behind the truck.

Our top speed in this truck because of the load was only 40mph, and it took us an awfully long time to get to that speed. We would be travelling along a seemingly flat section of road when he would shift down a gear or two as there was a slight incline, even though we could not see it.

We stopped at a place called Barrow Creek, where we had a couple of sandwiches and a cold fruit drink. Barrow Creek is an old telegraph relay station situated only 30 miles from the exact centre of Australia.

The weather so far has been beautiful, clear, and warm in the day and cool at night. We stayed at Barrow Creek for about a 1/2 hour, then pushed on. One thing I forgot to mention about this truck is that behind the seats is a sleeping compartment, and about 1 1/2 hours after we got in the truck, Paulene retired to this very comfortable area of the truck and remained there for the duration, sleeping most of the way.

The scenery on this part of the trip was quite monotonous, being a very flat and awfully dry country. It was interrupted south of Tennent creek by the Devil's Marbles. This is a big formation of huge round rocks in some very interesting formations. They look so out of place stuck out here in the middle of nowhere.

These truck drivers in the north are a very interesting lot, and they sure don't lack a sense of humour. Our driver told us about big signs that had been erected in the middle of nowhere. One had on it Tyndall's lumber yard, as this was where a driver named Tyndall had tipped over a large truckload of wood. At another place was a sign Jameson's Hamburger stand was now open. This was where a fellow had tipped over trailers loaded with buffalo meat.

At about 9:00 pm, we were about 20 miles from Alice, and the country was getting a little hilly, and the road was winding this way and that and up and down. This is where we saw our driver really handle this long and heavy load, it being a real joy to experience the skill first hand.

We arrived in Alice at 10:30 pm, unpacked our gear, and said goodbye to our Kiwi friend. Now we had to find ourselves some accommodation.

I slung my pack, and off we trotted, the centre of the town being about 3/4 of a mile away. Alice Springs being a real tourist town, we had a bit of trouble finding accommodation. After a bit of enquiring and a few phone calls, we found a motel. It was a bit expensive at $12.00, including breakfast, but we needed a good rest. It was a lovely motel, quite luxurious even, having a large swimming pool and beautifully appointed rooms. We woke up early the next day, and after a big breakfast, we both felt 150%.

Now, the road south from Alice to Port Augusta is gravel and dirt all 800 miles of it, so very few people take their cars over it; instead, they put their cars on the train, which runs twice a week on Sundays and Wednesdays. So, if worse came to worse and we could not hitch a ride, we would take the train to Port Augusta. Seeing we had two days before the next train, we would try hitchhiking anyway. We took a cab to the outskirts of town to a very pretty place called Heavitree Gap.

The Heavitree Gap, or Ntaripe in the Arrernte language, is a gap in the MacDonnell Ranges of Central Australia. It is the entrance to the city of Alice Springs, and in addition to the Todd River, it carries the main road and rail access to the South.

The Gap was and still is a most important sacred site for the Arrernte people of the area.

On 21 April 1886, The Heavitree Gap Police Station was established, which is of significance to the Northern Territory as the first permanent police base in Central Australia. Initially, the police station comprised bough wurleys and a tent for stores. By 1887 a thatched log hut had been added, and in the following year, an old hut from the Telegraph Station was erected for use as living quarters. Today, owing to flooding from the Todd River, railway construction, and use of the area for Telstra cabling, no trace of these early buildings remains.

There are old stories of non-law-abiding people that would travel 100s of kilometres to flee the south of the country, heading to the north end where they might escape the clutches of the police, only to be nabbed at 'Heavitree Gap' as it was the only way though to Alice and points north.

The morning was clear, and the sun would soon warm the air up. We both felt so good and happy we didn't care if we had to stay there a couple of days and take the train. But Paulene and I were being as lucky as we were with hitchhiking only stood in this beautiful little place for only 3/4 of an hour.

Paulene standing on the side of the road with our Perth sign waiting for a vehicle that might not come as most cars travelled the 800 miles south on the train rather than risk the awful track (as it was called).

A few cars went but were only Dept of Works people only going down the track a couple of miles. Then, a semi-trailer with two fellows in it went by but stopped up the road around the corner a few hundred yards. Both guys got out and started checking their tires etc. I decided to go and have a natter with them.

As I was approaching the truck, this big fellow looked up with a smile on his face. I asked him if he could possibly fit us in. He said, "We were just thinking about that." Just then, his mate came up, and they both looked at each other and then said okay, let's see what we can do. So, I ran back up the road to get Paulene her gear and my pack.

Now, here is how our new home worked out, the truck was a big International with a big flatbed trailer behind. On top of that trailer was another trailer just like it and on top of that trailer was a big Dodge diesel truck facing backwards.

This was to be our new home for 800 miles of dusty, bumpy, bull dust-covered track. You can see Paulene looking down from our perch high up in that cab.

I tied my pack on the lower trailer, and they gave me a big rug to wrap around it that would protect it from the dust. We then climbed way up to the top of our truck, and we were away.

The two drivers were German and, at this stage, seemed very pleasant and kind. Within a few minutes, we were off the paved highway and on the rough road, or as it is called a track.

We had only gone about 25 miles when there was a great rattling noise. They stopped and found that one of the spare tires had broken off. The smaller of the two walked back up the road a couple of hundred yards and collected it. But then further investigation showed us that we had lost not one spare tire that had broken loose, but two. Where was the other one? We sat and waited for a while, and a car driven by a couple of girls on their way to Ayers Rock happened along and told us the tire was 20 miles back. So, we turned around and drove back and collected our other spare.

By this time, we had more of a chance to get to know our new friends, and the more we talked to them, the more we liked them. They were both fine-looking Germans, quite aristocratic-looking. They also both were real gentlemen.

We drove on all day over a very rough track, but it was very pretty as the earth was so red and much redder than we had seen before. About three weeks ago, this area had received its first rain in 8 years, and little shoots of grass and plants were growing all over what had recently been a desert.

I can't help but think that someday they can bring and control the rains or somehow irrigate this inland part of the country. Australia is going to be very, very rich indeed. In this country that hasn't seen rain in 8 or 9 years, the cattle, what little there are left, have been living on lord knows what, and when the rains came, and a little grass grew, the cows did not know what it was and kept on dying needlessly of starvation.

At about 6 pm, we came to an outpost. (Whatever it is called now, it surely would not look the same as the highway is paved, and the fuel stops are pretty posh looking compared to the rough track we travelled over.) Here we filled the truck up with petrol and got ourselves some tucker to eat later on. All this place consisted of was a store, a police station, and the headquarters of a big station (farm). Also, at this little outpost, we picked up two more hitchhikers.

These two fellows were also German and had only been in Australia for nine months, so they didn't speak very good English. They had been at this place for three days and had not been able to get a ride; this will give the reader an idea of how much traffic passed through this remote outback. Mind you, they were a different class of Germans and weren't very well presented.

These fellows rode on the bottom trailer, spreading their sleeping bags on top of some canvas tarpaulins. At night they had a very cold ride as out here in the desert, the temp dropped like a stone at night.

So, within half an hour, we were on our way again. We only drove about 3 miles out of town to where we would build a fire and have dinner.

We built a big fire and watched a very beautiful sunset, and enjoyed a fabulous dinner and a billy of coffee that only an open fire in the outdoors can produce. We sat around the fire for about 2 hours, getting to know each other.

Our German drivers had both led very interesting lives; one had been a parachute instructor in the French Army when they were in Viet Nam and had spent four years in Saigon. Right now, he is making plans to return as he has had a fabulous offer there. We then got back on the track and again headed forever south. The track was terribly rough, and we had to go through some really bad washouts. This was our view as we drove through the desert, the fine dust roiling up behind us.

It was going through some really bad ones that we almost tipped over. It was so close that Kurt had to stop the truck; he was shaking so badly. We up top didn't realize it had been so close; all that happened was we got tossed about a bit and felt the truck swaying to and fro, but we thought we had just hit a series of bumps. If it had tipped over, we would have been in the worst possible spot.

In the way of wildlife, this evening, all we saw was one Kangaroo. At about 4 am, they stopped, and we had about 4 hours of uninterrupted sleep. We awoke with the sun and, in short order, were on our way again. We sat up in our perch, enjoying the scenery and the birds, which were abundant. About 4 in the afternoon, we were approaching Cooper Pedy, and we could see the scattered diggings not far from the road. Cooper Pedy is very famous for its Opals. Most people live right down in their mines, both to protect their diggings, and it would be cooler too. Big mounds of earth scattered everywhere with cars, trucks, or Land Rovers parked alongside.

In a few minutes, we rolled into the town itself, and what a surprise it was too. To say the least, it was wild and wooly indeed. There were a few scattered buildings around, the miners' store and bakery, plus a small hotel.

This was the scene as we entered Cooper Pedy in July 1966, dusty, very dry, and quite poor looking. Some folk got lucky and made big money here, but I suspect a lot did not.

There were also lots of Aboriginals around, the likes of which we had not seen before. They were much different than the ones we had been used to up in Darwin. The men had quite long matted hair that mixed in with their beards and cotton bands around their heads.

We attracted quite a lot of attention when we rolled into town and especially when Paulene and I got out of our truck cab way up on top of our load. We had to fill up the truck with petrol. Notice Paulene was still up in the top cab. The first thing I did was grab my camera and take some black and white photos, then change the film to colour slides. We then got down from our perch and wandered around a bit, and bought some more provisions.

The town is much more modern in today's world, with paved wide streets, modern well-built buildings, etc.

The town is much more modern in today's world, with paved wide streets, modern well-built buildings, etc.

We were almost tempted to get off here and try our luck at Opal mining. There are lots of stories of people coming up here for a couple of weeks and getting very rich. We stayed for about 3/4 of an hour and then pushed on.

About 2 miles out of town, we stopped and had something to eat, and this gave us a chance to explore some old diggings and collect some rocks with not quite mature Opals in them.

Then we again headed south, and as the sun was setting, we saw all kinds of Kangaroos; they were truly beautiful as they either sat up and watched us or hopped away and hopped they could too. Night came, and we kept driving, seeing a few more kangaroos by the lights of the truck.

We arrived at Port Agusta at 4:30 am and stopped at an all-night road stop. Our drivers had a feed, and we then said goodbye. The two German hitchhikers walked off toward town. Paulene and I went in and had a good wash, then sat down to a delightful cup of coffee. Over this, we decided what we would do next. We thought we would wait here until 9 am, then find a motel and have a good rest and leave first thing in the morning again.

Then we noticed a Falcon Station wagon pulled up with N.S.W. plates on it. I don't know why but I went out and asked them if they were going west to Perth... and they said yes. I asked if they could fit us in, and the driver said, "I think we can work something out." I went back inside to Paulene, not knowing really what to think, as I didn't particularly like the look of these two fellows.

One of them, the owner of the car, had a funny look in his eyes. I told Paulene and asked her to have a look at them; she didn't think they looked too bad, so we decided we might as well go. They came in for something to eat, so we had a chance to talk. They were both German too. The owner of the car was about 40, fairly tall and plump; the other guy was short and seemed very quiet. What happened next was a first as far as my hitchhiking experiences were concerned. He asked me to put our names and last addresses on a piece of paper so he could check us out with the local police. This he apparently did, and he gave me the paper back a little later.

Anyway, in 1/2 an hour, we were on our way again. I still felt a little uneasy about these two, and it was a feeling that was to prove itself and stay for the length of the trip. We made good time getting to Ceduna, which is right on the coast of South Australia.

Benny, the owner of the car, thought he detected something wrong under the hood, so we stopped, and he took the valve cover off and found not enough oil was getting to the rocker's arms. He and Wolfgang then proceeded to repair it the best they could, as all the garages were closed for the day. Because of a few showers of rain, we were there for about 2 hours, then were on our way again.

It wasn't far out of Ceduna that we left the bitumen and got on the rough gravel road that we would have right through to Norseman, 1202 Kilometers away. Benny drove for about 25 miles and then asked me if I would take over. I said sure, so I went up front with Wolfgang, and Benny went back and sat with Paulene. We drove and drove, and I watched the mileage pile up, and it was soon dark as we forever headed west. Wolfgang and I talked about everything from soup to nuts, and I found he is not a bad sort once you got to know him. Paulene and Bernie were talking away in the back, and it was later that I found out that he made a bit of a nuisance of himself from time to time, but nothing Paulene could not handle. (With her Karate skills). :)

About 8:30 we stopped in the middle of nowhere at a little way station and bought some petrol and filled our thermoses with coffee. I also purchased a boomerang at a very reasonable price, it being made by some aboriginals at a mission nearby.

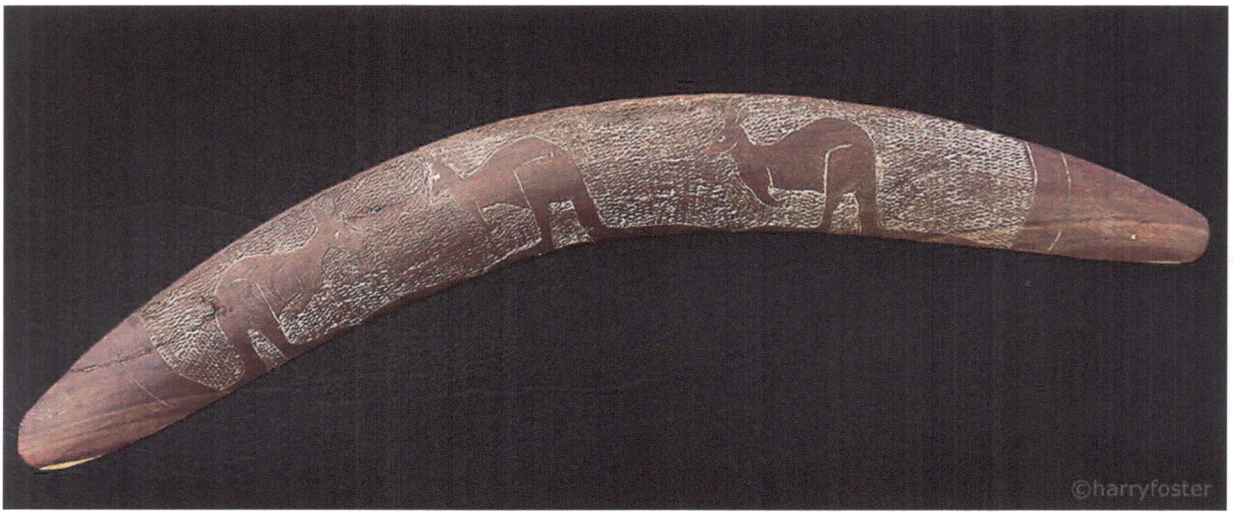

In about 20 minutes, we were on our way again, Paulene coming up front to join me for a while.

This is where I took advantage of a gift from the truck drivers we had from Alice Springs to Port Agusta. They gave me two small pills he called Stay-awake pills. I took one at about 9 pm while driving and did it work; I have never felt so awake. We talked and sang, and the miles kept rolling under us. The road was very rough, though, and our top speed was around 45 mph. I made a game of dodging the pot holes, which made things more interesting. There were also Kangaroos that were everywhere, and one had to be careful of not hitting those, too, as they sometimes jumped right in front of the car. These Kangaroos out here were big too, sometimes 6ft or higher and weighing up to 200 lbs; you don't want to hit one with your car.

About 1 am, I took the other pill that we had and kept driving and did so until around 5:30 am when we had to fill up with gas. We came to this roadside place that sold petrol, and it was in complete darkness and thought we might have to wait until later to get filled up. Wolfgang hammered away on the door, and finally, a voice answered. An elderly sort of fellow came out looking very sleepy-eyed and filled up our car, and then we were on the way again. Wolfgang took a turn at the wheel, and Paulene and I sat up front with him.

He didn't try and dodge the potholes but just drove through and over them; the springs and shocks bottomed out many times. Rocks were thrown up at the underside of the car so hard you thought they would come through. One time we hit a series of bumps, and there was a loud bang, and we all thought the car was falling apart, but it wasn't until we reached Perth that we noticed a hole as big as my fist right through the floor in the back seat area. We had not noticed it before as there was so much gear strewn around. Wolfgang drove until first light, and then Benny took over, and shortly after, we came to the Bitumen, which we would have through to Perth. We saw a few more Kangaroos in the early morning, but besides that, there was nothing except the never-ending straight-as-an-arrow road. It was about 10 am as we were approaching Norseman and the gas tank said empty, and Benny didn't have the Gerry can filled up. We must have been running on fumes, but we made it and pulled up at a gas station restaurant. There were no washrooms, so Paulene and I walked over to another place to have a wash and eat while Benny and Wolfgang stayed in the first place.

We had a good wash and ordered a nice breakfast when we saw our two guys heading over to where we were in the car. They pulled up and we waved at them; indicating we would be a few minutes; they then departed.

I thought they were just going to turn around as they looked a little impatient. I asked the waitress if she could make our meal to take away, but the guys didn't come back, and we waited and waited and started to wonder if they shot through and just decided to leave us there. We decided to wait an hour, and if they didn't come back, we would call the police. About 5 minutes before the hour was up, they showed up, and we were on our way again.

The car, by this time, was a real wreck and hardly had any power, but we plodded on. We arrived at Coolgardie around 1:30 pm.

Coolgardie being an old gold town is now virtually a ghost town. I photographed the Denver City Hotel with a 30-something car out front. There was lots to see in this old town, and we drove all around, seeing as much as we could. This shot shows what the hotel looks like now, all nicely restored.

Except for stopping one time to do some shooting with the 22 rifles they had in the car, the rest of the trip to Perth was uneventful, and we arrived at 10 pm.

We asked the guys to stop at a motel on the outskirts of town as we were in dire need of a good clean up. We were almost red from the Bull Dust of the Nullarbor Plain track, getting into our very souls.

We must have presented quite a picture, and as we approached the desk of the Motel and asked if they had a room. The fellow said, I'm sorry, but we only have the ambassadors' suite available. I said we would take it! The shower floor and walls turned red, and we got back to reality.

We did this hitchhiking trip of 2600 miles in 5 days for an average of 520 miles a day or 837 km.

We stayed in Perth for three weeks before our ship was due to depart for Naples, Italy. Our home was a dirt-cheap hostel with one 3ft wide bed and a hot plate down the hall. We did a lot of walking in those three weeks and got to know and love Perth too.

The ship we would embark on for a voyage of 5 weeks to Naples, Italy, was the T.S.S. Fairsky of the Italian Sitmar Line. We had stops and stay-overs at Singapore, Columbo, Aden, and a bus trip to Cairo, Egypt, to avoid going through the Suez Canal. She was requisitioned by the Americans in the 2nd world war and turned into an Escort Air Craft Carrier. After the war, she was returned to a passenger liner, though very small by today's standards.

Chapter Four

Our seven-week bicycle trip from Ottawa to Mexico in 1970

This trip came about because after meeting my future bride Paulene in Sydney, Australia, in 1965, then working our way around the world to Canada and getting married in 1967, I had yet to meet her family. We both had good jobs in Ottawa but decided to go to NZ for a year or two before coming back to Canada, settling down, and perhaps starting a family.

We didn't even have bicycles at the time we came up with this crazy idea, but we rented a couple one day and rode from Ottawa to Manotick and back (a distance of 24 miles) and thought, 'okay, we can do this'. Three weeks later, we were on our way. We did not get a shot of us as we left Ottawa, so the first shot of us on our bikes was taken in the States.

This shot of us on our bikes was taken as we rode into the town of Thornton, Indiana. On the trip, it happened a few times when a reporter from the local paper would track us down, take a photo, and do a bit of a story. Some were nice enough to write to my parents back in Ottawa and let them know how we were doing.

As the story says, we were 19 days from Ottawa at this stage, tanned and fully acclimatized to our days of riding.

The Fosters ride through Indiana, 19 days out from Ottawa. —The NEWS Photo, John Flora

Pedaling To Mexico

By JOHN FLORA, Staff Reporter

THORNTOWN, Ind. — Mr. and Mrs. Harry Foster passed through here yesterday on Ind. 47.

What's unusual about it is that they're bicycling from their home in Ottawa, Canada to Mexico City where they'll take a plane to visit Hastings, New Zealand, to visit Mrs. Foster's parents.

Most people who take the Ottawa-to-Mexico City trip miss Thorntown, but the Fosters are picking their route on a day-to-day basis and happened by this way.

Sitting astride his 10-speed bicycle, Foster, 28, explained that he and his 26-year-old wife, Pauline, plan to pedal their way to Mexico City within six weeks and then fly to New Zealand.

"We left Ottawa 19 days ago," said Foster, a photographer on leave from his post with the National Museums of Canada.

"We've been averaging about 58 miles a day since we started. Our best day was 85 miles and our worst day was 30 miles—rain," he said.

Foster explained that he met and married his wife four years ago in Australia and soon returned to Canada, without meeting his new in-laws.

"We prefer to camp," Mrs. Foster said, "but we have stayed in motels twice since we left."

After spending the night camping in a rest park south of Frankfort, the couple planned to reach Danville, Ill., by the end of the day.

"We don't have any definite route to Mexico City. Every morning we look at the map and decide which way to go. We're just picking our way across the country," he said.

Foster's bike is laden with about 70 pounds of gear, including a tent, saddlebags and a small red and white Canadian flag on the back. His wife's bike weighs in at about 50 pounds, loaded.

"The people have just been fantastic," Foster said. "The police, too. Whenever we get to a town in the evening and don't know where to camp, we go to the police station and ask them. They've always been more than helpful."

The Fosters said they plan to spend about two years in New Zealand before returning to Canada.

Sept 14, 1970

Day one of our bicycle trip from Ottawa to Mexico. What a fabulous day for our departure from Ottawa; the morning donned bright, clear, and cool. After a few tears were shed saying goodby to my family, we departed at 7:30 AM, down Kent St from McLaren to Wellington, then left for the beautiful scenic Ottawa River Parkway. We no sooner got on the parkway when Paulene, in tears, signalled me to pull over. She said the bike felt weird, and she could not control it nor feel comfortable riding it. I must have looked a tad grey at this stage, not 30 minutes into our seven-week trip. I redistributed the weight on her bike, putting more forward, and this solved the problem.

We took the parkway to the western end of Ottawa, then on to Carling ave, and then to Highway #7. We had a real good day of cycling, considering it was our first, and covered 116 kilometres. This took us to the Silver Lake provincial park.

We set up our tent right down at the water's edge, nestled in amongst a group of trees. This little tent was ordered from the Eaton's Catalogue and only cost $32.00. It lasted for this trip of seven weeks, all our tramping trips during three and a half years in New Zealand (we did add a fly in NZ), and our seven-week canoe trip on the way back to Ottawa. No trouble with the bikes today, but Paulene had a sore knee, so we taped it up, and she used my shoulder to get about the site. The next morning she still could not walk comfortably but was ok on the bike peddling. :-)

A couple of things we found out today was that dogs took a great interest in us, often chasing out after us or barking themselves silly. The other thing was buses. On a two-lane highway like this, when they went by at speed, we would almost get blown off the road, and the big transport trucks were almost as bad. So now, when I see one of these vehicles in my mirrors, I would signal Paulene, and we would ride on the shoulder, taking us a bit further away from them.

At the campsite, there was an English couple on a new BSA Lightning motorcycle. Their plans were to travel all over the continent for three years without working. Somewhere along the way, they picked up a little dog who was now riding with them and keeping the girl warm.

Our expenses today consisted of the following, $1.00 for two milkshakes and two chocolate bars, .30 cents for a Coke and two peaches, and $3.60 for our supper and breakfast groceries. $4.93 or less than our allotted budget of $10.00 per day. The odd time we will go over is when we stay in a motel sometimes.

Our little Swedish camp stove is the best bargain of all, so quick and efficient, even running on ordinary gasoline.

Sept 15, 1970

Woke up this morning to the sound of rain on our tent, a beautiful sound but not too good for cycling. It soon let up, and we were able to start the day. A big hearty breakfast of cereal, eggs, toast, and coffee, and we were on the road at 10:30.

It rained lightly for a couple of hours before the sun broke through. We did not get as far today as Paulene's knee was quite sore. If we were walking, we would not have gone a mile, but it did not bother her nearly as much when riding. Later on, the rain came down heavier, so we stopped and donned our ponchos.

These economical Ponchos worked surprisingly well in keeping us dry when riding or taking a break, as Paulene is doing here.

We sat in the rain for a bit and then continued riding, ponchos and all. Paulene being still sore and the thought of setting up and taking down a wet camp, we decided to stop at a motel. It was just west of the Skootamatta River; the motel now called the Unconventional Moose. We rented a little cottage for $10.00. We had a big supper at the nearby Two Bears restaurant for $3.30.

It was called that, as for years, there were a couple of bears in a cage beside the restaurant. Buses that travelled between Ottawa and Toronto always used to stop here so folk could watch the bears. Changing mores over the years dictated that was just not acceptable anymore. Our only other expenditures were .30 cents for four chocolate bars and two milkshakes at .35 cents each, bringing our total for the day to $14.85. Our average now being $9.89 per day. Our mileage today was 74km, making our daily average now 95km.

BUSTER & BANDY - ACTINOLITE, ONTARIO

The bears loved their Coca Cola and ice cream and on their cage the sign actually said something like 'our favourite foods are Coca-Cola and ice cream'. It was said that sometimes they would drink up to 30 bottles on a hot summer day. I remember them pacing back and forth in the cage and wondered what kind of an existence they had. The family said they were "rescue bears" The bears were found as orphaned cubs and knew no other life and probably would have died had they not been given homes. So what happened to them? The bears lived into their 30's and just passed away of old age. Teddy, the first of the bears died first. Of the two bears everyone loved, Buster died first and then Bandy – missing Buster I guess.

Sept 16, 1970

Awoke this morning after a good night's sleep. A cup of tea and a piece of toast to get us on our way. What a day it was, too, no rain but a 40 kph wind right into our faces, and those hills, the endless hills in this area. Some we even had to dismount and push our bikes up. Paulene taking a break here, upside down in a ditch, must ask her if she remembers why she did this.

Paulene's knee is feeling better with the elastic bandage in place, but one just becomes physically exhausted fighting the elements, hard to even talk to each other over the wind while riding.

We can't get over the dogs. The farmhouse can be fully a kilometre back from the road, and still, the dogs will see or hear us and kick up a hell of a racket. We stopped at a little grocery store in the afternoon to get our food for the night and breakfast for the following morning. An old timer came out of the store to talk with us, he seeming most interested in what we were doing. After talking for 10 minutes or so, he asked us if we would like a couple of fresh rolls that he had made this afternoon. Of course, we answered in the affirmative, so out he came with these beautiful rolls heaped with butter. A friendly old chap which was a taste of things to come regarding people as we travelled. Quite a few of the truck drivers wave or just give us a friendly blast on their horns; some in cars wave also. We always greet the survey crews and Hydro gangs, who are all very friendly.

We stopped and made camp at a little Indian River campsite just east of Peterborough, and a nice little place it is too.

(Now it is larger scale RV park.) When we first arrived, the owner's son of about 11 rode over on his bike and proceeded to ask us about a million questions. He could not get over how light everything was. He even came back later when we were cooking supper and could not believe that little stove of ours would really work. Today we travelled 74 km, so our average is 90km per day. Our expenditures were a bit higher today because of Paulene's bandage, a total of $10.90, so our average is now $10.23 per day.

Sept 17, 1970

Today dawned a beautiful day, cloudy bright, perfect for riding. We broke camp at 9:10 am; the owner's wife came over and said she hoped we would come back and see them on our return from New Zealand. Paulene is getting a lot stronger; he knees and shoulders don't bother her so much. She decided today to count the number of dogs that barked at us; the number totalled 29. One place we passed, there was a little puppy in the driveway wagging his tail while an older dog tied up started barking. The little dog looked at him, then turned back towards us and started yapping too.

Another time we stopped in this little country town of Leskard, where we would get some fresh fruit. While Paulene went into the store, I rode her bike down a side street, checking out a noise. I had just got 100 meters down the street when this great big husky-type dog saw me. By the look in his eye, I thought for sure he had me in mind for his next meal. He did not bite me, but he kept up a torrent of fierce barking right beside me as I rode carefully back to the store. I got off the bike, and he immediately shut up. I no sooner sat down on the steps of the store with Paulene, and this dog with tail wagging came up and proceeded to lick our hands and faces. About 10 minutes later, we mounted up and proceeded to leave town. You guessed it; the dog came too. He ran ahead of us on both sides of the road, in and out of the ditches, having a great time, us thinking any moment he would turn for home. After a mile or more, I had to literally chase him home, even throwing small stones his way. I'm sure he would still be with us if we didn't chase him back.

It was a good day for cycling, though, except for lots of hills, about seven that we had to push our bikes up. A few friendly people today, again, those who waved and those who were interested in what we were doing. In the late afternoon, we arrived in Port Perry on the shores of Lake Scugog. After asking someone where we might put up our tent, he said follow me, and he took us to a place where he thought we might be allowed to. However, it turned out the park was closed. We were just deciding what to do when the rain started to come down quite heavily, and that sort of put a damper on the tent idea. Someone else directed us to some little cabins, and that's where we stayed for eight bucks.

These little cabins made our daily expenditures go way up. Today it was $13.99; our average is now $10.99 per day. Our mileage metre finally gave up the ghost, and I'm sort of glad as well. Now we enjoy it a lot more and don't worry if we have gone as far as yesterday. Now we just cycle all day and look for a place to make camp at around 4 p.m.

Sept 18, 1970

Well, we had a relaxing day today as our ride from Port Perry to Newmarket wasn't too long; we often stopped to relax and take photos, arriving in Newmarket around 2:30 p.m. in the rain. We have good friends in Newmarket that we were going to stay with for a couple of days.

When I was a young lad of 18 living in Richmond Hill, I worked at a Texaco gas station part-time. Another of the part-timers was a fellow named Jim Barnett. He was like a mentor and second dad to me. After some time, he suggested I apply for a job where he worked full time, a place called Vickers Sperry Rand, an English company making hydraulic power plants to do everything from operating lift bridges to stamping machines in the auto industry. I got the job in December of 1962 and stayed there until 1965, when I sold everything and headed off to work my way around the world. The job was great at Vickers, and I learned skills that would stand me in good stead all my life. The trouble was they tested me six ways to Sunday and had my career path all planned out. I was not ready for that just yet. Here are a few photos of Jim from later in life. Paulene and I were best of friends with Jim and his wife as long as they lived, living the last 25 years or so in Huntsville, Ontario. Me on the left, then Dave Lavery (a friend from Vickers), and Jim on the right. What a friend!

The Barnett hospitality is something that has to be experienced to be believed. They put on so much food and such good wholesome food too. We stayed up swapping lies till about 1:30 am before hitting the sack. Our total expenditures today were $2.00 for our lunch and a couple of cokes. This brings our average down to $9.34 per day.

A great but busy day today. First, the great big Barnett breakfast, then Jim and I went out in the truck to get a load of sand for a friend of his that does plaster work. After that was finished, Jim worked on his truck & car most of the day, and I worked on our bikes, cleaning and oiling everything. I also got a basket for the front of Pauline's bike so that we might carry our groceries for the evening meal. This cost us .79 cents. Bought Jenny some hand cream and chocolates for $5.50 and a case of beer for Jim at $2.62, and some postcards for $1.00. total outlay today was $9.91. The daily average is now $9.43.

This evening we had quite a get-together with a couple of the fellows that Jim and I used to work with at Vickers, Al Jackson and Dave Lavery and his wife, as well as some other friends of Jim's. A real good time was had by all, finally wrapping things up around 2 am.

Sept 20, 1970

Up at 7:30 am this morning, rather Dopey and tired as we didn't have much sleep. Left Jim and Jennie's at 10 a.m. in a head wind, so it was rather hard going for the first few hours, but it finally eased, and the sun came on beautifully in the afternoon. We didn't need to walk up too many hills today, but it is still certainly not rolling plains. For lunch, we stopped on the side of the road and made ourselves a couple of delicious tomato sandwiches with a Coke, finally reaching Georgetown around 5 p.m. We were quite tired, and Paulene's knee was hurting quite a bit, but it's the left one now. With a bandage on, tomorrow should be fine. Inquired as to campgrounds and found ourselves 5 miles away from a rather good one, although, for $2.50, washing facilities were poor. Paulene has been adopted by the camp mutts. One stole a plastic bag with the delicious home-cured bacon a friend of Jim's gave us. Got that back in a hurry and had that for supper with wieners, peas, tomatoes, and cucumbers. Very tasty. Our total expenditures today were $6.23. This brings our daily average down to $8.99

Sept 21, 1970

Got a late start this morning and didn't get rolling till 10 a.m. it was a bad day for cycling as the wind was right against us the whole day at 20 to 25 miles per hour and very hot at 85 degrees Fahrenheit; we made it to Kitchener however and are staying at a beautiful campsite. The highlight, or should I say low light of the day, was when we stopped for a coke at a BP service station restaurant. We stayed about 15 minutes then we were away again, but I forgot our camera bag, complete with $950 of camera equipment, passports, visas, etc. We got one and a half miles away when a fellow in a truck stopped me and told me I'd forgotten the bag. So off I headed at about 60 miles per hour, and just as I was pulling into the lot, the owner was pulling out as he was going to start after us. This was so very kind of him. That was quite enough excitement for the day. All in all, we are being received very well by people we meet along the way; they are all very Interested in what we are doing. Our expenditures today amounted to $6.54 plus $2 for the campsite total of $8.54; our daily average is now $8.93.

Sept 22, 1970

We enjoyed a good day of cycling today even though, like always (it seems), we were dealing with a headwind. The good thing, though, is we seem to have passed the real hilly country we had been going through. There were a few this morning, but after Stratford, it really levelled off nicely. We had to ride right through the heart of Kitchener this morning and found it a most interesting City, much more industrialized than I had imagined. But that didn't seem to take anything away from it, as it had a definite character all its own. We didn't really see enough of Stratford to say anything about it, as the highway pretty well skirted it. After Stratford, we just sailed along. We stopped, though, to make our lunch alongside the highway at some stage. This is a real treat that we look forward to all morning. We like to have a couple of tomatoes and cheese sandwiches and perhaps a cheese and jam one too.

At 3 p.m., we arrived at a fabulous-looking park right near Saint Mary's, Ontario; we still felt like riding, but the park looked too inviting, and it would give Pauline a chance to wash a few clothes as well. We set up our camp in a bit of a drizzle, but the sun came out a little later, and I took a bunch of pictures around the camp and down by the water.

Later on, while I started getting caught up on the diary and Pauline was reading this morning's Global Mail, this old chap came up from the only other campsite in the park that was occupied. He stayed talking with us for about half an hour. He was Dutch and had been in Canada for quite a while, but he still had a thick accent. He was a nice enough guy, though, with some well-thought-out ideas on life. Supper tonight is going to be a big stew with extra vegetables and some fresh tomatoes. Our food buying and meal preparation is working out well. We buy what we need for supper and breakfast in the late afternoon just before we make camp. Our expenditures today amount to only $6.50 as we didn't need to pay for the campsite; there was no one there to collect any money. Our daily average is now $8.66.

I mentioned the Dutch fellow earlier; well, he came back as we were preparing supper and said he would try a little fishing off his boat. He only did that for about 20 minutes when he came back up, as his car was parked near our tent. He stopped to chat again and stayed on through our supper until just about dark, telling us all about his family and just about anything he could think about. I thought he seemed a bit lonely. After he finally left to go back to his camper, darkness set in, and we were all by ourselves. I was set for a real good sleep as the time was around 8 p.m. Then Pauline said she thought the place was spooky; I, being surprised by that, asked why she said that man gave her the Spooks and she figured he was a bit nutty and reckoned he would come back in the night and shoot us. Well, this really threw a screw in the works, as I thought he was an ok guy. I started racking my brain, thinking about all we had talked about. Paulene reminded me about the movie that we saw not long before we left on our bicycle trip. The movie was called Easy Rider that featured a couple of Rednecks who had rifles in the back of their truck window and ended up killing two guys on a motorcycle. Paulene thought about that movie and how this guy also had rifles in the back window of his truck. So that sure put my plans for a good sleep on hold. Normally I would have been asleep by 8:30, but I arranged my sleeping bag so that my head was at the door and could better open the flaps if need be, and I lay on top of my bag and not in it, waiting for the boogie man to come back.

I listened to 1 3/4 baseball games on the radio until 1 am, and I could no longer stay awake. It was pouring with rain, and the spiders were seeking refuge in our tent, and I had finally had enough of trying to stay awake, so I closed up the tent and fell asleep. We both woke up at 7 a.m. Paulene said that she had a great sleep, mine not so much; it certainly was a night to remember! During the earlier part, around 9 to 10 p.m., we'd be lying there when all of a sudden, Paulene would squeeze my leg and say there's something out there. She said this a few times, and each time I would poke myself out of the tent, look all around and discover that the noise had been a leaf falling on the tent roof or some such silly thing.

Sept 23, 1970 — 10th day out

What a day today was, our best day of cycling regarding distance covered, travelling 137 km right to Sarnia. It was fantastic; the roads were flat, with no wind but quite a bit of rain. We just sailed along mostly in 9th gear. We had a little break in a small town for an ice cream cone, then stopped for lunch at the 45-mile mark and did the last 40 miles straight into Sarnia. We were on the road from 9:20 am till 4:45 pm, averaging a shade over 19kph, including stops.

We arrived and followed signs to a KOA campsite, pulled in to find there was only one car and trailer there beside us.

We set up our camp not far from them and weren't even finished when a fellow came out the door and shouted for us to come over and join them for cocktails when we finished setting up. When I was in registering and talking with the owner of the campground, this fellow from the trailer came in to register also, and we all had a good chat. After I had returned to our tent, he came over and formally invited us to supper. We spent a fabulous evening with these people, a Mr and Mrs Paul Baker of Pensacola, Florida. They were kind, friendly, and such good fun to spend some time with. He is a retired Navy type, still quite young and just travelling all around the country. They wanted us to get in touch with them when we got to the Mexican border, and they would meet us there, and we could travel together while in Mexico. The campsite is quite nice, with the facilities the best we have seen yet. Tonight we did a huge wash of just about all our clothes. Our total expenditures today were $7.80, our average is now $8.58 per day.

Sept 24, 1970 — 11th day out

Said goodbye to our new found friends and hit the road at about 10 am. Got straight on a four-lane highway that led to the bridge that crossed to the States. We had to push our bikes over the bridge as they wouldn't allow us to ride over.

It is quite a large bridge, and it took us 3/4 of an hour to get over. It was quite pretty from the top as one could see the vast expanse of Lake Huron and, on the other side, the chemical industries area of Sarnia and the very blue waters of the St Clair River flowing beneath the bridge. One thing that I forgot to mention was that I had to dispose of some Hash that was given to us in Ottawa on leaving. Not really knowing how to use it, we never did, and not wanting to be caught bringing it into the US, I flushed it down the toilet at the campground. We arrived at US customs to be met by an extremely friendly customs man. We were through in a flash, with good wishes from the customs officer.

We rode through Port Huron and immediately noticed the difference between the States and Canada, even though there was not 1 mile separating the two. In the States, almost all the houses were of frame construction, while in Canada, most houses are of brick. Besides the tangible differences, there was just a very real feeling of difference. We finally got pointed in the right direction and headed west on a four-lane decided highway that was to narrow down to a two-lane after 6 miles or so. The four-lane was great as we could ride side by side on the paved shoulder/ It's really a shame that we can't use these highways more often.

We didn't push ourselves today, and did only about 38 miles taking us just past Imlay city. We were caught a couple of times in the rain and the last time was just 1 1/2 miles from where we were going to make camp. We took shelter under some trees but still managed to get fairly wet. Finally, the rain subsided, and we got on our bikes again and just started out again when the heavens opened up. We kept going though and finally arrived at our campsite. We decided to stay at a State roadside park not intended for overnight camping. There were beautiful big pine trees everywhere, and we were the only ones there.

It was a soggy camp as it rained some more during the night. We just wrapped all our wet clothes in a plastic bag and put them in a saddle bag so to dry another day. Paulene heard a few more people in the night stopping, and every tine the wind blew, an avalanche of water would come down from these stately old pines. The people we have met so far have been extremely friendly. People here seem very open and are always coming up and talking to us and wishing us well. One restaurant even had a special guest book they asked us to sign. Our total expenditures today were $7.01; our average is now $8.43 per day, with a total so far of $92.76

Sept 25, 1970 — 12th day out — Entry by Paulene

Today was a rather uneventful day except for the fact that we did 98 km. We headed west from Inlay City to Lapeer and then started south, finally making camp at a State Park called Highland Park. Michigan State parks are much like our Provincial Parks. Just as we were trying to locate the camping area, we flagged down a car to ask for directions. In the car were two drunk squirrel hunters with accents from the deep south and missing a number of teeth. They told us how to get there and parted, saying they would see us later as they were staying there also. We did not need another night of me standing guard, so we tried to put our camp in a part of the park where those fellows were unlikely to find us.

We did have a very persistent visitor during the night, though, and that was a raccoon. After supper, we were playing cards at the picnic table by the light of our candle lantern when we heard a noise very close by. I grabbed a flash light and shined it in the direction of the noise and discovered the Racoon, not 4ft away, trying to get into one of our saddle bags. I chased him away in short order and shortly after went to bed. I was no sooner tucked into the sleeping bag when we heard a noise at our table. Quickly unzipped the door and shone the torch outside. There he was, perched on top of our food cache, preparing to dig in. I yelled and hissed at him, but he just looked at me like I did not matter. So, I had to don clothes, shoes, etc., and go after him. he wouldn't leave the table until I belted him on the back three times with the flashlight. He got the message and left. No sooner than I was back in bed, the raccoon was down out of the tree and back at our table. This time, however, we fooled him as we took all the food into the tent. We slept surrounded by yogurt, honey, butter, bread, bacon, and eggs, and we were quite cramped, as you can imagine. Total expenditures today were $7.10, average now of $8.32, and the total spent so far is $99.86

Sept 26, 1970 — 13th day

Because today was a miserable-looking day, and both of us felt like a rest, we decided to have a short day and only go to the Pinckney Recreation area, a mere 25 miles away. The park is 11,000 acres and sits at an elevation of 922 feet. Our short day turned out to be a real dandy as the wind blew and the rains came down, and we didn't get to the park until 5 o'clock, wet, cold and miserable. We had a devil of a time finding the camping area and had to ride about 6 miles on wet gravel roads that played hell with the bikes. We finally made camp on the banks of Crooked Lake in a small, lightly wooded campground overrun with young boy-scouts. Even saw two young bicyclists from Ann Arbour, Michigan, with full camping gear.

As it was the weekend, there were lots of visitors there, and it seemed really homely. All while setting up camp and during supper, it rained off and on, making life a tad miserable. We had a great sleep, though, as the temp went down to 45 degrees, and we woke with the sun. The total outlay today was $6.70 average daily now $8.20, and the total so far is $106.56.

Sept 27, 1970 — 14th day out

Didn't get away today till 10.30 as we are going to have a short day and stay in a motel. We woke up with a beautiful sun that dried things off in about 1.5 hours. A chilly night but we had one of the best sleep of the trip so far. The highlight of today was just about an hour after we set off. We were still within the boundaries of the State Recreation area when we came upon as sign saying. Louie's Big Game Shooting preserve.

I couldn't believe my eyes, but there was a lot of shooting coming from back in that property. Curiosity was driving me crazy, so we stopped at the first gas station, and I went in and spoke to the owner, asking him what Louies Big Game preserve was all about and what kind of animals could you shoot. He said that, first of all, it costs you $100 just to get in the gate, and you can shoot Buffalo, Elk, Moose, Deer, etc., etc. He said it perhaps had some underworld connections but was not sure.

To us, this whole idea was seemed incredible; who would go and shoot some big game animals in a place like this? It would be like shooting fish in a barrel. Imagine shooting Buffalo, Elk, or Moose 40 miles from Detroit. I did a little research later and came up with this.

Louie's Big Game Shooting preserve

In Michigan---Open all year round. No licence required. Wild Boar, Corsican Ram, Fallow Deer Elk, Sika Deer, Buffalo, Whitetail Deer, Mouflon Sheer, Aoudad Sheep. Daily kills guaranteed, Write for Brochure.

Going back a little, though, as we were leaving camp and for that matter, ever since we got up, we could hear gunfire from all directions. One fellow parked his car near our tent and got out with a gun, and strode off into the fields. Now all through this recreation area, there are foot paths linking other lakes and points of interest. All kinds of people use them, from scout groups, families, and young couples. There were also hunters carrying high-powered rifles, shotguns, and lord knows what else. We must have passed 20 cars parked in an area no more than 3 miles from our campground and also a picnic area at another lake. To top it all off, we had to do a little pushing up steeper gravel hills to get out of the area.

Hunters everywhere, gunfire everywhere. We felt lucky to get out of the area alive.

We finally found a motel at a place called Clinton, 38 miles south. We booked in at 3 pm. First of all, we did some laundry back in town then I did a half-pie cleanup and re-oiling of the bikes. We spent a relaxing evening watching TV and reading the newspaper. Our total outlay for the day was $21.50, bringing our average up to $9.14 per day and a total for 14 days of $128.06

Sept 28, 1970 — 15th day

We left Clinton at about 9 am and headed south towards the Ohio border. A good day for biking as the wind is from the North West, and that makes life a lot easier. We got to within 6 miles of the Ohio border when Paulene got a flat. I took the wheel off and found a fair size gash in the tire. So, I put a boot in the tire as a safety measure and then a new tube. (I will fix the other one later) I then pumped about 45 lbs in with the hand pump, enough to get us to a service station where I could bring it up

to 60 lbs or so. We came to a station in a bout 1/2 mile, and they had an air line but no gauge, just straight from the compressor. I found out later it was 120 lbs. I gave the tire a good shot, and before I could even disconnect, the tub blew up "POW". So 20 minutes later, we were off again, having put another new tube in Paulene's bike.

We soon crossed the border and stopped to take a photo of the occasion.

We liked Ohio from the start. Quite a few cars in Michigan would honk at us, and some drivers would yell at us to get off the road, which was most unnerving. Here in Ohio, folks would give us happy waves, and when we stopped, people would come up to talk; really friendly and so noticeably different from Michigan. Perhaps this was because we are going further into the country and away from the built-up areas around Detroit; it sure is nice, though. As it was very cold and there were no suitable campgrounds around the town of Napoleon where we decided to stay, we booked into an inexpensive Motel. The gas heater was broken, but finally, a repairman came and got it going again at about 8.30 pm. We went into the town to have supper and buy a few things; everyone said hello and wanted to hear about our trip. The people of Ohio are the friendliest we have encountered since leaving Ottawa. Our outlay today was $14.50, our total now $142.56, and a per-day average of $9.50.

Sept 29, 1970 — 16th day out

We left the Motel at 9.15 and headed west along a scenic trail that would take us to Defiance, Ohio, 17 miles away. It was a lovely ride; this Ohio farm country is something else, the land is flat, and all you can see in some places from horizon to horizon is corn, the highest corn we have ever seen, much taller than I am. The houses too are all beautiful with the gardens so well kept. The impression is one of great prosperity.

It was not the greatest day for cycling, even though it was a beautiful day. The wind was coming out of the south west, and we were heading south. We changed our tactics a bit today, which makes it a lot easier for Paulene. I now ride in front and break the wind for her. She also feels less lonely there as she can see me where she could not before. We just kept going south all day along Route 127 and finally stopped in a town called Van Vert. We were staying at a lovely campsite about 2 miles out of town. While Paulene was in a grocery store, about four people came up to me for a chat, including a gentleman in the Lincoln Continental, who was most interested in our story and talked for about 15 minutes. Our outlay today was $6.11; our average is now $9.21, and the total is $146.67. Our mileage to date is 757 miles. Something I did not mention was we are now using our stove in the day time also. Today we stopped in the morning and heated ups our Billy and made a cup of coffee, and did the same at lunch time. It boils the water so quickly. All kinds of people wave and honk their horns as they see us by the side of the road, eating and having our coffee.

Sept 30, 1970 — 17th day

We didn't get a very early start today as it was 10.15 before we headed out, but the wind was on our side for a change. We had as our goal a town called Portland, which is in Indiana, approximately 50 miles away.

It was a real good day, having an enjoyable lunch by the side of the road after doing about 33 miles. We arrived in Portland at about 3 pm and went directly to the police station to ask them about camping facilities around Portland. We have found the police to be most helpful and very receptive. They told us of a place about 8 miles out of town on highway 67. We had a hard time getting away as they wanted to talk, being very interested in our trip, and insisted we send them a card at the completion of it. We headed south from Portland to where I thought the campsite was. It was a great highway, and we had just sailed along at a great old rate, and it wasn't before 14 miles had passed that we realized we had taken a wrong turn. What a spot to be in, nowhere to camp, and the nearest town of any consequence being 15 miles away. So, off we headed me with my tail between my legs for having made the mistake. This time the wind was against us, and we also ran into the first hills we had in 3 days. We finally arrived in Albany, and a policeman directed us to a campsite 4 miles away.

Some very nice people ran this campsite which was not the greatest, but we were happy. We set up quick as dark was setting in fast. There was a pile of wood nearby, so we had a lovely fire for about 3 hours, and this cheered us up a lot. Our outlay today was only $4.70, the lowest yet. Total now $157.37 and an average of $9.02 per day. Our mileage today was 80 miles, so our total now is 837 miles.

As I write this, I did send the Portland Police Department an email today, April 19, 2020, (only 50 years late), that we had safely finished the trip to Mexico,, but worth doing, if only for a chuckle.

Oct 1, 1970 — 18th day

We had a real good day today with very light winds from the east, then changing to the North as we are heading west; this is alright. We went 80 miles today. We had planned to only go as far as a town called Tipton, Indiana, but it was still relatively early when we arrived, and we were a long way from being tired, so we headed on to Frankfort, where we planned to stay in a Motel. We arrived in Frankfort at 6:30, only to learn there was no accommodation left as there was an antique show in town. One Motel owner gave us directions to a campsite 4 or 5 miles south, so we headed out there in a hurry. We went 10 miles and still hadn't arrived when we were to a state roadside area with a grocery store across the road, so that is where we stayed. There was a house backing right into the park, so we felt quite safe.

Our lunch break today was at an A&W in Elwood. As we pulled in, a couple of college-looking guys in a car yelled out, "Where you headed?" I said New Zealand. He answered, "That right?"

We made our order and sat down. About 10 minutes later, these fellows came over for a chat. Apparently, one of the fellows thought I was just being smart when I said New Zealand, the other thought it was possible, so they came over to find out for sure. They were great guys, and we had an interesting conversation. They thought it funny that a couple going all the way from Ottawa, Canada, to New Zealand should happen to go through Elwood, Indiana. Later on, when we went through the town of Tipton, we had to stop for a red light. Some kids happened to be there, one yelling over, "Where have you come from"? I said Ottawa, Canada. One of them was so surprised he said "is that right, I just can't believe it!" That was priceless.

One thing I forgot to mention was our late start to the day; we did not get away until 11 am, but we still managed to do 80 miles by 7.30 pm. Our total mileage is now 917 miles. Our outlay today was $5.95, the total now 159.32, and the average daily cost is now $8.85. Must send a card after the trip to the owner of the campsite we stayed at last night Mr Russ Hunt River Bend Campsite, Albany, Indiana.

Oct 2, 1970 — 19th day

Out on the road to day at 10.00 am. We had a real good sleep, and everything remained dry, which was a welcome relief. We headed for a town 28 miles away against a real stiff head wind. We just can't say it enough, but the people are just too friendly. One young and pretty woman stopped us on the highway to ask us about our trip and to wish us well, and for the second day in a row, an older fellow (a different one each day) on a motorcycle rode alongside us, just talking to us. Just after we passed though the town of Thornton, a guy on the side of the road waved us over. He had a camera around his neck and waved us over, and introduced himself as a reporter for the Indianapolis News newspaper. He was a nice guy and, in a few seconds, pulled out his notebook, wrote down the whole story, then took a couple of photos of us riding by.

We reached Crawfordsville at 2 pm, bought a few things for lunch then headed out to the other side of town. We went three miles and then had lunch, all the while realizing the wind was getting stronger. We headed out anyway, the next town was 24 miles away, but we thought there would be a Motel before then. We wanted a Motel because I hadn't had a shower for four days. Anyway, we travelled about 4 1/2 miles before realizing the if we went even 1/2 MPH slower, we would stop. We asked someone how far it was to a motel, and he said 16 miles. There was no way for that, so we headed back to Crawfordsville. We had the wind behind us and arrived very quickly. We booked into a Motel the was just perfect, right next to a big shopping mall where we could get some more essentials, food sunscreen, lotion etc. Our faces and legs are getting brown as berries. Our mileage today was 42 miles;

this brings our total to 959 miles. Our total outlay today was $18.13; the total now is $177.45, and an average of $9.34.

Oct 3, 1970 — Day 20

Well, today, we will complete our first thousand miles. Before heading out today, the sky was almost blackened by a flock of starlings that reminded me of living in Hudson, Quebec, when a young lad. It was a fabulous sight as the sun was just coming up, and the birds were calling out to each other. The sight and noise is something to behold. We got on the road at 8 am, and even that early, we had a stiff headwind to ride against, and as the day progressed, the wind got stronger and stronger. For sure, the wind is our worst enemy. However, slow and steady wins the race on a day like today, and we just kept pedalling along. We reached Danville, Illinois, by 2.30 and the Kickapoo State Park, 7 miles west, by 4.30 pm. This was not long after crossing the border between Indiana and Illinois.

Paulene was saying earlier in the day how she was no longer scared of the dogs that ran out barking at us on occasion. And then… a little black long-haired rascal ran out and bit Paulene on the ankle. He broke the skin, and Paulene thinks she will have a good bruise. In Perrysville, a very small town, we stopped to buy lunch at the general store, which in itself was so interesting as one could hardly move for all the stuff inside. It takes the record for sure. Our total mileage today was 52 miles, bringing our total to 1011. Costs were $5.60, total now $183.05, average $9.15.

Oct 4, 1970 — Day 21

Well, we had our first frost last night, but we still had a real comfortable sleep. We had on our snuggies and blue socks and a sweater on our feet and on top as well... besides our ski Jackets. One would think that with all this on, we would be uncomfortable, but no, we slept like babies.

There was a big family near us that were very friendly, and we talked with the father for quite a while, telling stories.

The sun came up big and warm, and it wasn't too long before things dried off. We finally got on the road at 10 am and headed west again. This being Sunday and after our hard day yesterday, we decided to make this our day of rest and only go around 33 miles to Urbanna and booked into a Motel. Just as well, too, as we were both tired and couldn't have gone much further. We arrived at 2 pm and enjoyed a restful afternoon watching TV, reading the Sunday papers, and eating. Our outlay today was $18.90, the total now $201.95 or $9.57 per day. Total miles now 1044.

October 5, 1970 — 22nd day out

We got an early start today. This is usually the case when we stay at a Motel. We rode right through Urbana and Champaign and liked what we saw; it seemed like a well-integrated area. We saw whites and blacks together all over, kids included. It was the first time we saw school kids mixed. One young black boy rode up beside us on his bike and wanted to know all about us, where we were going, and where did we come from. When I said we were from Ottawa, he said oh yea, up in Canada. We felt this was pretty good coming from a ten-year-old black kid when some of the older white people didn't have a clue where New Zealand was.

Then we got out into the country and headed west. Well, there was one heck of a wind from the south that made things just miserable. It must have been 20mph with gusts higher. Paulene really hates the wind and does not enjoy these days at all. It makes me sad when I look in the mirror and see that pained expression on her face. However, we just kept on going and found if we talked a lot, we sort of forgot the wind, and the time went by quicker.

We finally reached Lincoln by 4.15 and were lucky as there was a campsite 1.5 miles from where we asked a garage owner if he knew of any. So, it was not a bad day in the end, as we went 66 miles against that wind. Our total mileage is now 1110. Our expenditures today were exactly $10.00, a total now of $211.95 and an average of $9.63 per day.

Oct 6, 1970 — 23rd day

Had a great sleep last night, but before going to bed, we had a real good visit with another young couple. How it started was the owner of the campground found out we were going to New Zealand and had found out that the male half of another young couple had been to NZ. He told the couple about us, and we soon after got together and had a real enjoyable evening of coffee and wine. They were both teachers who were off to Costa Rica, where they hoped to teach English for a year. They were travelling in a Volkswagen bus that they had set up as a camper. A very nice couple who we wished the best in their adventure.

For the first 40 or 45 miles of our run today, we had a tailwind, and what a difference that makes. It's so enjoyable as it does not feel like work at all and the miles keep rolling by. Just before lunch, we came to a hill, the first in a long time. When we reached the top, we stopped and decided to have a coasting race, and while we were racing down the hill, Paulene had a flat tire. We decided to have lunch then and there, and while Paulene was fixing lunch, I was fixing the tire.

Shortly after, we headed due south, we only had to go in that direction for 11 miles, but it was the worst 11 miles of the whole trip. The wind was right on our noses and so strong and steady. Even I broke down and cursed the bloody wind today. But we did this cursed 11 miles and then changed direction and did the final 11 miles into Beardstown. Seventy-three miles today, which brings our total to 1183. We stayed at a motel tonight as there are no campgrounds, and it was not far off being dark when we arrived. Our cost today was 12.83, a total of $224,75 averaging $9.77 per day.

Oct 7, 1970 — 24th day

Got off to an early start today, and we weren't sorry to leave this Illinois River Valley area at all. The people were a little different and hard to explain but seemed to sometimes look right through you and were less likely to engage with you. There seemed to be a palpable difference between the people we had met so far on higher ground.

As we climbed out of the valley and went a few miles, everything seemed to return to normal, like this farm scene.

We were lucky today as the wind was almost at our backs, sometimes on our side, which made cycling a lot easier. We joked and laughed our way along, and the miles just rolled by. By the time we stopped for lunch, we had travelled 47 miles. People in cars, trucks, and tractors always wave and spur us on. We stopped in this one town just before lunch, and Paulene went into a store to get some bread when this real old pickup truck stopped directly behind us, and an old and wiry fellow got out and said, 'can I come with you?' I talked with him for a while, and Paulene came out and joined the conversation. He asked us where we were headed, and we told him NZ. He was very surprised and then asked us how far we had come. I said just over 1200 miles. That really knocked him over, and he looked and said, 'that's why Mom has such big muscles'. That had to be the funniest remark of the trip so far.

Another funny thing happened today (funny now but embarrassing then). This happened around 12 noon. We came to a little town, and as we were going through, Paulene noticed a Dairy Queen-type store, so she said let's stop for ice cream. We parked our bikes and got our cones, and sat down in a couple of chairs. As it came up quite windy, it wasn't long before the wind blew Paulene's bike over with a big crash. I went over and picked it up again, and it wasn't a minute later it blew over again. There were a few people parked around and three women in the store, so red-faced, I went over, picked it up, and moved it to a different position. Then we just stood there finishing our ice cream cones and being ready if her bike started to fall again. Would you believe it, but my bike got blown over and fell right through a 3 ft square window with a loud crash and tinkling of glass. I immediately went over and offered to pay for the window to be replaced. The girls working there would have none of that and said the insurance would pay for it. They turned out to be very friendly and kind, and we enjoyed a few giggles about the situation. They then suggested it might not be a bad idea if we were on the road before the owner returned.

We finally arrived at Quincy on the banks of the mighty Mississippi river at 4 pm and booked into a KOA campsite. Just after we finished putting up our tent, I went over to a nearby trailer to ask how far it was to the nearest grocery store.

They said it was a fair distance away and offered to drive us. So Paulene and this kind lady took off to the store while I sat and had a beer with her husband, Bob. This couple are entertainers who travel all over the country and usually spend 2 to 3 months in a town. She plays the piano and sings, and Bob plays drums and sings too. Such friendly people, who invited us to supper (Paulene, Bob and Alma outside the trailer), and what a great visit we had.

We talked about everything under the sun, with much laughter and carrying on. They took a couple of pictures and gave us a polaroid picture of ourselves. They had to leave at 8 pm as they work from 8:30 am to 1 am each day at a local nightclub.

Their trailer is an Airstream, one of the streamlined ones that is built like an aircraft. It had all the luxuries of home and certainly was comfortable; every square inch of space is used for something.

Our cost today was $11.30, as we bought enough groceries for tomorrow as well. We have not had to pay for the campsite yet, so that will go on tomorrow's sheet. Our total now is $236.05; our average now is $9.84. Our mileage today was 64, our total now is 1247, and our average for riding days is 52 miles per.

Oct 8, 1970 — 25th day

Had a good night's sleep and woke up at about 9 am. What a good feeling it is to wake up and know that we don't have to peddle off. We just lazed around for the morning then Bob and Alma called us up to their place. They took us out and showed us all over town to all the points of interest. Being a river town, it has a very old history, and some of the houses were majestic, so large and posh. They took us to the club where they were playing and introduced us to the boss, and gave us a tour. They even played a couple of the numbers they performed and did a super job.

These folks are just too much; we all get on so well together. We had supper with them again, and at 8.15 pm, they were off to the club but said we would be more than welcome to stay and watch TV and make ourselves something to eat, etc. As the weather was really stormy, they even insisted we sleep in the trailer tonight; they had a spare double bed that they folded out for us.

Their engagement finished at 1.00 am, and were home shortly after. When they arrived, Alma made us some Tacos, which are a Texas treat, and so we enjoyed these no end and talked till 3 am, and we all folded.

Never have we met such kind and generous people in our world travels. They sure made us extremely happy. Our total outlay today was $5.40; the total is now $241.45, daily average is $9.66.

Oct 9, 1970 — 26th day

We sure slept well in the trailer last night. We awoke at 9 am and sneaked out so as not to wake Bob and Alma. We made breakfast and then went up to the KOA office to do some laundry. We met the manager and his wife for the first time, and they, too, were so kind and friendly. They gave us a bunch of postcards that, anywhere else, would have cost us a dollar or more. They also said if the weather got mean again that we could sleep in the lodge.

While Paulene was doing the laundry, I was writing postcards. While we were busy doing that, the manager's wife called up the Quincy newspaper, telling them about us. Pretty soon, a reporter and photographer came out from town. They took some photos of us riding our bikes as well as a nice one with our bikes at the campsite and got some details of our trip so far.

This was all very exciting for us, and we managed to get a plug-in for Bob and Alma as well.

We spent the rest of the day with Bob and Alma, just talking and talking. They wanted us to sleep in the trailer again, but as the rain had passed, we decided to sleep in the tent as we didn't want to be getting too soft. We did spend the evening in the trailer watching TV again and taping the Tom Jones show for Bob.

Bob and Alma came home early again, and spent some time with them before retiring to our tent. We were only charged $2.50 for three days at the campsite instead of $3.00 per day as the owners admired what we were doing and just because they were too kind. Our total outlay today was $4.00; the grand total so far is $245.45, an average of $9.44. Something I forgot was that Bob and Alma are picture-takers, even taking one of us in bed.

Oct 10, 1970 — 27th day
Paulene writing

I had a nice sleep this morning, the sun was up, and Harry was up pottering around. After breakfast, around 9.30, Alma and Bob came down and watched us packing the bikes. We then had coffee with them, and after lots more picture-taking, we very sadly farewelled each other. We were all so happy together, and it seems sad we won't be able to visit with them for so long.

Finally left at 12 noon, our latest start yet. A 20-mile trip to Hannibal just across the Missouri border. We crossed the Mississippi River, which, true to form, was muddy. Hannibal is famous for being the boyhood home of Mark Twain, which we went and visited.

A proud Paulene standing on the bridge spanning the famous Mississippi River

The famous fence that Tom had his friends whitewash while he sat back and supervised

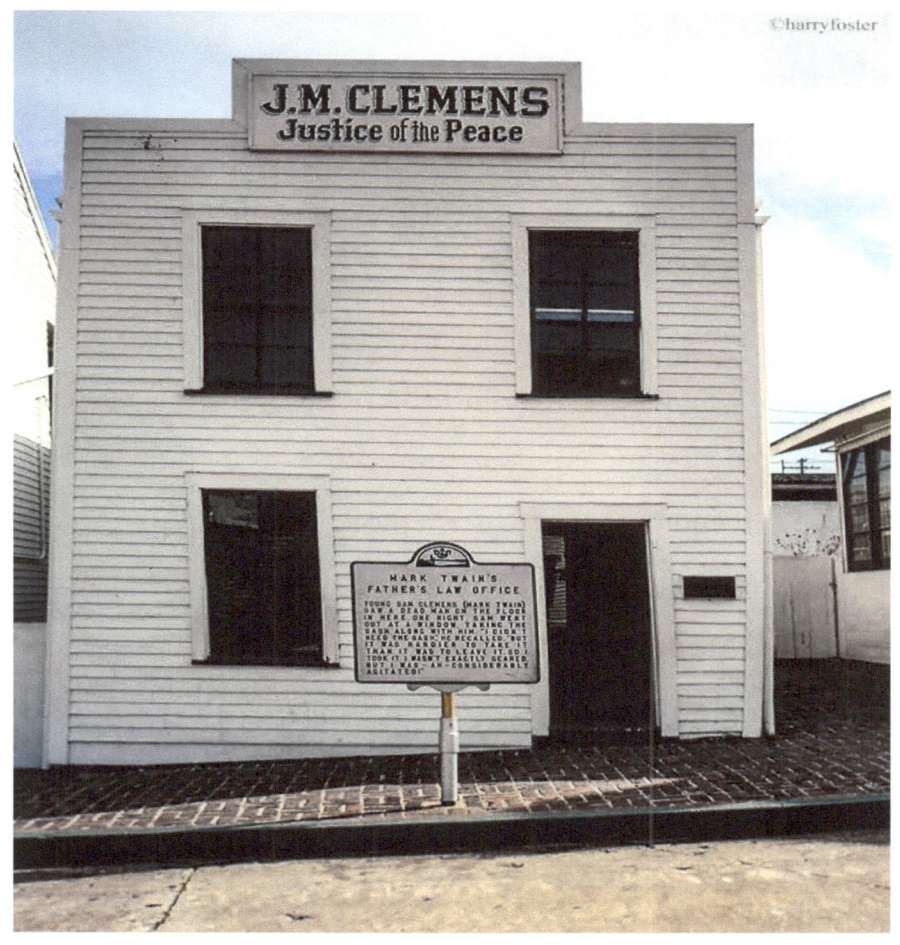

The office of Mark Twain's father, in Hannibal Missouri

The most interesting place was the Museum, which we would have liked to spend more time in as it was packed with fascinating things to read about. Before leaving Hannibal for the final run of the day we stopped at a restaurant for a hamburger and milkshake. We left for Monroe city 19 miles west. It was getting rather late, but we made a great time and arrived with plenty to spare before dark. We stayed at the BelAir Motel. Did some shopping for tomorrow and had supper in a restaurant as there was a no cooking sign in the motel. The cost for the day was $22.70, the total now $268.15, an average of $9.93. Mileage 41 miles, total 1288.

October 11, 1970 — 28th day
Paulene writing

My favourite kind of day as there was no wind. The sky was clear and blue, and the ride was effortless, up until Macon, anyway. But after Macon, hills not too steep, though. But Sunday drivers, that is another issue. We will be glad to have our truck drivers and regular highway travellers back tomorrow. We had our lunch in a lovely spot next to a stream, complete with a little boy fishing for catfish. We even rode our bikes through the stream, as it was only about an inch deep. We finally arrived at Brookfield at 5 pm and decided to take a motel as the days are short now, we don't have as much time to make camp. Tomorrow we shall leave early as there is a State Park 63 miles from here. The folk at the motel are very kind and let us cook supper on their picnic table. They even gave us a fresh pot of coffee. Our costs today were $12.75, total now $280.90 average now $10.03. Mileage today was 75 miles total, now 1363.

October 12, 1970 — 29th day

We kind of crawled out of bed this morning as we felt all nice and cosy. But there was a campground just past Cameron 71 miles away, which we wanted to get to, so we had to get cracking. With a friendly wave from the Motel owners and a farewell bark from their dog, we were on the road at 9 am.

All day the road was like a giant roller coaster. We shot down one side and got halfway up the other before having to peddle. Photo of Paulene taking a break on top of a hill.

However, we both started to get a few aches and pains in the knees as we had been having nothing but flat roads lately, so not used to these hills.

Surprise, surprise, we actually bumped into someone we knew. About 10 miles west of Brookfield, with much waving and honking of horns, a Lincoln and Airstream trailer pulled along beside us. It was some people who had camped near us at the Quincy KOA. They stopped, and we had a chat for a time. They are going in the same general direction as us, so we might just meet them again. We had lunch with a couple of Wasps at a roadside table and even met a man who had been to New Zealand.

Instead of staying at eh State Park, we found a private campground 7 miles south and 1 mile west of Cameron. It was a nice park, but it will be very nice when the mud dries up. There is a little lake that is filled with some sort of fish that make one hell of a splash when jumping. We had supper and sat around a nice campfire during the evening. Our costs today were $11.05, a total now of $291.95, an average of $10.07. Mileage today was 71 miles, so the total now is 1434.

October 13, 1970 — 30th day

Well, we really like our campsite, and in a year or two, when they get all the grass going. it will be really nice. They have the lake stocked with Carp and Catfish; the largest catfish caught so far is 42 pounds.

Our ride today was difficult as, again, it was like a roller coaster all the way. We had hoped to get to the other side of Kansas City, but we decided we would get tied up in rush hour traffic, so we thought we would stay in a Motel. As we were headed through the Northern Part of the City, we stumbled across a campground. We couldn't believe our good fortune as who would expect a campground right in a city?

We are really noticing all kinds of changes as we go further west. One just needs to go into a supermarket and see all the different foods strongly influenced by Mexico. The people's accents, too, are really beginning to sound great. As always, the people are really friendly to us and can't believe it when we tell them how far we have come; they just stand with their mouths and eyes wide open.

Paulene on the open road

One thing that I forgot to mention was it snowed three days ago where we camped last night. A real storm that lasted for about an hour. Our costs today amounted to $11.02, total now $302.97, average $10.10 per day, and our mileage today was 49 miles, total now 1483

October 14, 1970 — 31st day

Paulene writing

We are now in Pleasanton, Kansas, a long way from Ottawa now. We left Kansas City, Missouri campground at 9.45 and then put in the hairiest 2 hours of the whole trip so far; it sure was for me anyway. We travelled through Kansas City on the expressways and Turnpikes, where the traffic was so fast and thick. So many roads weaving in and out and around. From one side of the city to the other was 22 miles, and we were really travelling fast. The road early in the day was hilly, but we had a good tailwind, and after lunch, it flattened out a bit.

Later in the day, the countryside became very green with rolling hills and little lakes. Pleasanton is very rundown and looks like in another two years; it will be a ghost town. Our costs today were $13.20 total, now $316.17, average is now $10.19. Today's mileage was 77 miles bringing the total to 1560.

October 15, 1970 — 32nd day

Didn't get on the road till 10 am as we were just having a short day. The idea is to just go to Fort Scott, where there is a KOA campground. There I will clean and re-oil the bikes etc.

It was a real great ride of 26 miles; all said and done. Fort Scott is an old town with a lot of history. The name of the town is from a fort that was built in 1842 when they were having trouble with the Indians. It was used a little later when the Civil War came along. The town itself has a lot of old buildings, and half the streets are still of cobblestone.

In the afternoon, I cleaned the bikes up and, while doing so, found that I had two broken spokes in the rear wheel and Paulene had one. Our tires are also getting badly worn, especially the back ones. I think we will stop in Oklahoma City for a day, and I'll rotate the tires and perhaps put our spare on mine.

Today while buying groceries in Fort Scott, a reporter from the local paper came along and got down all the details. It's funny, but I guess one gets wise. Paulene was checking prices on different items while I was on the grocery cart when I noticed this fellow come around the corner and down our aisle. I just knew he was from the newspaper. He came out to our campsite later on in the afternoon to get a picture of us, our bikes and tent, etc. It was getting pretty late in the day by then, so not sure how the photos would turn out. We had him promise to send a copy of the paper back to my parents in Ottawa. Costs today were $10.60, total now $326.77, and the average is now $10.21 per day. Mileage now 1586

October 16, 1970 — 33rd day

Happy Birthday to Paulene today!!!

We both woke up this morning with cold feet. What a night, it must have gone down to the high 20s as there was an extremely heavy frost, everything covered in furry white. I took some photos both in color and B/W while Paulene peered out from the depths of her sleeping bag. We wouldn't have been cold at all, but we forgot to put sweaters on our feet... so they got cold.

Seeing the frost was so heavy when the sun finally burned through, everything got wet, and consequently, we were very late in getting away. We had a hearty breakfast of special natural health food, hot cereal, eggs and tomatoes, and milky coffee. We finally started peddling at 10.45. We decided to head south rather than west. We will gradually swing westward, then south to Tulsa, Oklahoma, then pretty well straight south for Texas. One thing I forgot to mention was that at the KOA, they had wall-to-wall carpets in the washrooms and even showers. That was a bit of a shock at first, but there they were, and it sure was nice to stand on a warm rug while in the shower.

Being Paulene's birthday, we went out for supper and had as much as we could eat of Sophisticated Chicken (whatever that was), and was it good. Even so, our costs today were only $14.98. For the next week, we plan to stay at Motels as we want to cover a lot of miles, and we can only do that if we get away early in the morning and not having to wait for our tent to dry. For this last part of the trip, we would like to keep our costs under $15.00 per day. That will give us 20 days to finish and remain within our budget. The total cost now is $341.75, an average of $10.36. Mileage today was 67 miles total, now 1653.

October 17, 1970 — 34th day

On the road this morning at 8.30. It was a good day for riding as the wind was very light. We covered the first 20 miles in record time. As a matter of fact, we got to Coffeeville by 11.45, and that was the 35-mile mark.

Coffeeville is one of the most famous Western towns in America. This was where four members of the Dalton gang and four civilians met their fate back in 1892 when the Daltons rode into town and robbed two banks. The two banks are still standing, in fact, and the alleyway where the famous gun battle took place has been restored to exactly how it was. There is also a museum there with all kinds of artifacts belonging to the Daltons and also artifacts of the day. A most interesting museum, which we spent about 1.5 hours exploring.

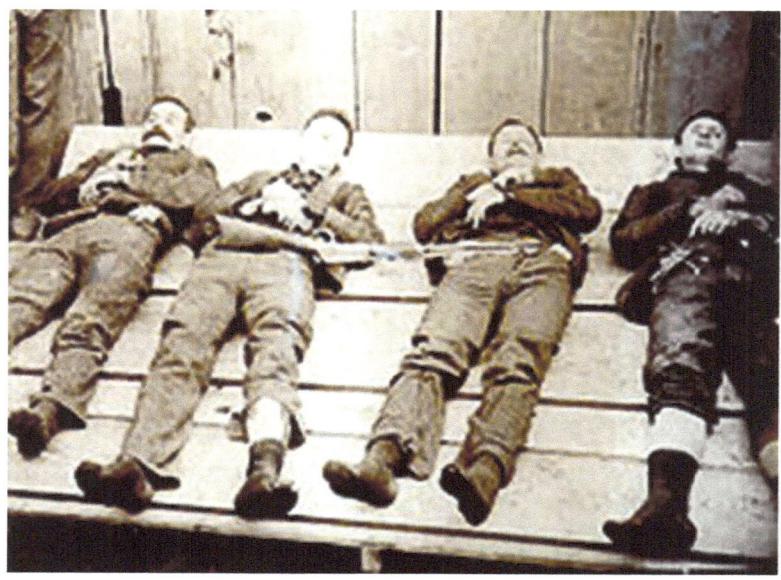

On the road again and crossed into Oklahoma three miles from Coffeeville, stopped to take a couple of photos, and had lunch shortly after.

It was only 23 miles to the next town of any consequence but a long way to the next, so we stopped at a town called Nowata, an Indian town, and there were sure a lot of Indians about. Just as we pulled into the motel, a girl went by on a horse, and it just looked like this was the way she went everywhere. Our costs today were $15.45, total now $357.20, average of $10.51. Mileage today was 58, total is now 1711.

October 18, 1970 — 35th day

Paulene writing

We had a good start today and were away at 8.30. Four hours later, we were at Tulsa, covering 50 miles, our best time, I think. The road was not flat either, but we had a bit of a tailwind and lots of good spirit. We passed through Will Rogers' hometown of Oologah; he being famous as a Cowboy, philosopher, and humorist. We are definitely in Cowboy country, with lots of cattle in the fields, and it looks like we have left the corn behind. Not as many places for me to pee without that corn.

Riding through Tulsa was another repeat of Kansas City, riding the freeways. The minimum speed is supposed to be 40mph, so we don't need to worry as we almost reach 50mph ;-) I think we are just so anxious to get it over with and escape from the traffic. It was a very warm day as well. Tulsa is very modern, with lots of hotels, restaurants, and modern apartment buildings, and obviously very prosperous.

Well, we got through alright, then rode on to the next town, Sapulpa, where we stopped at a handy motel. Well, what a dump, so cold and smelly, no TV, and Sunday afternoon is Harry's footie game time. Well, it was only $5.00, so we spent quite a lot on food to restock our larder.

In the evening, we walked to the local movie house to see the "Savage Wild" set in the Yukon; quite good. Sad to read in the local paper that the FLQ had murdered

Pierre Laporte in Quebec. Would love to get ahold of a Canadian Newspaper. Costs today were $13.39, total now $370.59, average 10.38. Mileage 68 miles, total now 1779.

Oct 19, 1970 — 36th day

On the road today at 8.45. The countryside was really reminding us of Australia, the earth being reddish and the trees almost looking like gum trees. Almost everywhere were oil rigs and their see-saw-style pumps. Photo Credit to Alex Burke.

Not sure why I did not take photos of these. The pumps come in all shapes and sizes, some powered electrically and some by gas or diesel engines with one cylinder that operated so slowly that one thought it would surely stop.

The roads today were all hilly, but as there was no wind, they did not slow us down too much, only a couple that we had to walk up. We covered about 45 miles before stopping for lunch near a few of these oil rigs. We then finished off our day in an easy fashion ending up at a town called Seminole, 77 miles from where we started. It was a real fun day with lots of laughter and horsing around. Our expenditures today were $14.36, total now $384.95, average now $10.70, mileage now 1856.

Oct 20, 1970 — 37th day

On the road today at 8.45, and right away, we realized it would be a hard day. There was a headwind with gusts up to 20mph and hills almost all the way to the town of Sulpher, where we were headed. We just kept plugging away, however, talked and teased each other, and the miles rolled by. At one stage, we came to a fence that had eleven Coyotes strung up on it, most looking fresh. We also started seeing different dead animals along the road, such as Armadillos and snakes that looked like rattlesnakes. Late in the day, Paulene called me back to look at a spider. This was like no spider we have back in Canada, being about 4 inches across with a large crowned black body with a light brown part at the back and very furry too. It was a tarantula. I turned him over to see two big clamp-like teeth. While taking photos of him, I had to keep moving him to where I wanted him to be. This made him mad, and believe it or not, he chased me, so I left him alone then.

We arrived in Sulpher at 5.15 and saw a Motel Hotel advertising hot mineral baths. We figured this was just what our tired bodies needed, so we decided to book in regardless of the cost. Well, the baths were out of commission, but the room was luxurious and the bed super comfortable, and the TV worked well, so it was all worth it. Our costs today were $19.70, total now of $407.91 and an average of $10.94. Mileage today was 62, total now 1918 miles.

Oct 21, 1970 — 38th day

Paulene writing

We slept in this morning; consequently, we were late leaving and had another strong headwind, so we did not go far anyway. During the night, someone stole my blue turtleneck and Harry's blue and black turtlenecks. None of them were at all valuable, and we just thanked our lucky stars; there was nothing on the bikes really precious to us. I hope the thief makes good use of them, as they were pretty well shot. I saw my first cotton growing today, and already we noticed lots of cacti. We saw a deer farm and the smallest whitetail buck Harry had ever seen. He was really cute, as he kept wanting to lick our fingers. Posted some more postcards today. We are staying at another KOA tonight, and I must say not very posh. The washrooms are of the usual high quality, although no carpet in the showers. As we arrived, a busload of men stopped in also. They questioned us on all aspects and angles, all greatly interested. By the way, we are now 9 miles south of Ardmore, Oklahoma. Our total expenditures today were $9.50, bringing our total to $414.21, average now of $10.90 per day. Miles today 45, total now 1963.

Oct 22, 1970 — 39th day

Had a good sleep in our tent last night, and in the morning, I went in to do my ablutions. The lady at the desk called out and said we had a call from the Fort Worth, Texas TV station WBAP NBC, but it was late at night, and she figured rightly that we would be asleep, so they asked that we call them to collect in the morning. I went back to tell Paulene with much interest. So, after we had finished breakfast and wrapped up our camp, we went to the KOA Lodge, and I phoned Ft Worth and talked to the newsroom. They want us to call them again when we reach the edge of town as they want to do a story about us. I told them we should be there tomorrow sometime and looked forward to seeing them. We got on the road at 9.45, and it was the hardest day of the trip; we were heading directly into a 20mph headwind and spent the whole day in our lowest gear. We were ready to call it quits after 35 miles, but there was nowhere to stay, so we had to continue on for another 23 miles. I took a picture today that I hope to sell sometime. There was a sign in a field, a big sign saying Welcome Marietta, stop here, and you'll stay. Right in front of the sign was a dead Hereford cow. I took both b/w and colour shots. Not long south of Marietta, we came to the Texas border.

This was very important to Paulene as Texas always seemed like somewhere from another planet for a girl from far off New Zealand. Our campsite was a bit barren, and the wind continued. This photo shows how we coped with the wind, creating a barricade of picnic tables and putting our cooking stove into a trash can.

Costs today were $11.83. Total now $426.04, average 10.92, mileage today 61, total now 2024. We are staying in the town of Dayton, at the top of the golden triangle.

Oct 24, 1970 — 40th day

Started out late this morning as a bad thunderstorm moved in and kept us at the Motel until noon. The rain came down like in Darwin, Australia, and Paulene said she had never heard such loud thunder. When we got out of Denton, we realized that the wind was almost as bad as yesterday. It was only going to be a short day as we are going to stay in FT Worth. On the way, another of my spokes sprung, and that brought to 3 that were broken in my rear wheel, so we had to find a bicycle repair shop. Just as we were entering the outskirts of town, a fellow in a pickup truck waved us over to the side of the road. He offered to give us a lift to the other side of the city so we wouldn't have to go through the Mixmaster, which is Ft Worth's highway system. We thanked him very much and told him we had to go to a repair shop and so would be staying here tonight. He then bought for a second and told us of a bicycle shop near his motel not far away. He was an Oklahoman who was working on a construction project here.

The people in Texas have been extremely friendly and open to us. Anyway, we went to the bike shop, and it turned out it was called Foster's. It was run by an older chap and a very friendly fellow he was. He was not really equipped for our kind of bike, but he was most helpful and really wanted to somehow help, and could he ever talk? He called another shop and found they had what we wanted, so off we went for a couple of miles to this other shop. We just pulled in, and the owner came out and said, "Bring your bikes right in." He had to make the spokes, and he then replaced them and gave us four spares. He even realigned my rear wheel, and he would not take a cent from us. He just said, "I'm glad to help you down the road." I phoned the TV station from the bike shop, but as it was late in the afternoon, they said they would have to do it in the morning. So off we went, determined to get to the south side of town so we could get a good start in the morning. That meant we had to go through the MixMaster during rush hour. That's something I would not want to do again; as it was, I ended up with a belly ache. We stayed at the Fort Worther, which is a posh motel on the freeway. Yes, we splurged; it's nice to do it once in a while. The total cost today was $17.20, and the total now is $443.24, an average of $11.08. Miles today 41, total now 2065.

Oct 25, 1970 — 41st day

Paulene writing

Well, we would have had a good start this morning, but after everything was packed and set to go, it was discovered my bike had a puncture. All the tools had to be unpacked, and Harry fixed it. Everything packed up again, back on the bike, and the tire was flat again. I must get a new mechanic. We finally left around 9.30. We had phoned the TV station to say we were leaving at 8.30 and would see them on the road somewhere. Well, with the late getaway, we missed them. Rather sorrowful day for me as I had my hat down over my face too much and didn't see Harry stop ahead of me. Crashed into his bike. I then had another puncture in the front this time. By this time, Harry was thoroughly cheesed off with our bad luck. We finally limped into Hillsboro around 3.30, and my back tire was flat again. I smelt moth balls as we entered the town. The highway is 2 miles from the town, and it looks a little forgotten. The motel is terrific, though, as we have a kitchen with fridge and stove and all for $6.00. Tacos for supper, and Harry changed my tube and tire, so hopefully, everything goes well tomorrow.

Lots of black folk in this town, and it seems very well integrated. We have been received by the blacks extremely well; from the start, they always having a wave and a big smile and are very eager to help. Costs today were $12.36, total now $455.60, an average of $11.09. Mileage today was 55, total is now 2120.

Oct 26, 1970 — 42nd day

Off again today into the wind, but it's only a short day to Waco, Texas. We have to get Paulene's rear wheel tuned up and a new tire fitted. Our day was only 35 miles long, and we arrived before lunch and booked into a cheap motel, and enjoyed an afternoon of football and relaxation. We didn't even have a flat today. Our costs were $9.86, total now $465.46, average $11.08 Mileage now 2155

Oct 27, 1970 — 43rd day

Well, today, as far as riding is concerned, had to be one of the worst. For a starter, we had a headwind that felt like a hundred miles an hour, the temperature was 85, and the humidity was unreal. Our day wasn't particularly long in terms of mileage, but it sure was in other ways.

We finally realized today that some of the things I said and did that I thought would encourage Paulene on down the road had the opposite effect, in fact, and just upset her and made her go slower.

One exciting thing that happened today that could have been a real disaster but turned out okay was as were riding along the shoulder of the IH35; there was a truck stop and restaurant ahead on a little grassy rise. As we approached, a big truck came down from the restaurant over the grass and jumped a 5" curb and then across the southbound lanes and across the median and came to a stop, almost completely blocking the northbound lanes. It was only then that we realized that there was no driver in the truck, and it was a runaway. A few minutes later, the driver came out of the restaurant, and there was one hell of a commotion. About 3/4 of an hour later, the truck went by, and the driver waved cheerfully.

We arrived at the KOA at Belton at about 5 pm, unrolled the tent, and then realized that we had left our tent poles. Luckily this KOA had trailer tents for rent. So we got one of those for the night for a couple of extra bucks. There were quite a few people camping there, and what a friendly bunch they were. Two of the people camping there had seen us at a rest area earlier in the day when we stopped for lunch. One of the men was born in Winchester, Ontario, and his wife was born in Australia. So there was much talking done with these and other people during the evening, and we spent some time watching the best color TV we had seen, a Zenith. Costs today were $9.43, Total now $474.89, average $11.04, mileage today was 46, total now 2166.

Oct 27, 1970 — 44th day

Paulene writing

Today was fantastic. We rode 110 miles and were still singing at the end of it. We left around 9 am with a north wind blowing. We didn't really believe it would last all day, but it did and even got stronger as the day progressed. We stopped for lunch after about 50 miles and then decided to stop at San Marcos, but we were feeling so good (Paulene biking along looking good), so we decided to do over 100 miles.

So, here we are at New Braunfels, originally settled mostly by Germans in 1845. We had a great supper at a German restaurant and felt really happy tonight. We are only 30 miles from San Antonio now. As we were preparing to leave the KOA this morning, Harry spoke to a man who had seen us in Frankfort, Indiana. It's a small world. Costs today $18.88, total now $496.77, average $11.29. Mileage today is 110 miles and our best yet. Total now 2276.

Oct 28, 1970 — 45th day

An easy day of riding today as we only had 36 miles to San Antonio. Everything started falling into place. A young Mexican gas station man put us on to a Motel just a 15-minute walk from downtown and at only $8.00 a night. It turned out to be the nicest motel we had stayed in. It had colour TV that really worked well, a radio on the bed as well as controls over the bed to operate all the lights and air conditioner and heat. There was even a sunlamp on the ceiling of the bathroom. The motel people were extremely nice and helpful and even suggested we keep our bikes in the room.

After a clean-up, we headed downtown to take care of some business. First, we went to a bank to get a draft we were carrying changed into Travellers checks and a cashier's check to cover our airfares to New Zealand. Well, they whisked us through in a matter of minutes, and everyone was so friendly and helpful. Next, we went upstairs in the same big building to a travel agent and in about 1/2 hour walked out with our plane tickets, just like that.

We then wandered around for a little, and I showed Paulene the Alamo. (I had seen it previously when a friend and I had hitchhiked right around America when we were 16 years old) but we were saving a visit there until tomorrow.

We no sooner got back to our Motel than we had a phone call. One of the other guests of the Motel was a salesman for a big American bicycle company and wanted to talk to us. He came over and spent an hour or so shooting the breeze. A very nice guy who hails from Tennessee. Through contacts of his, he arranged it so we could get two cartons that we could ship our bikes in from Laredo. Today's costs were $20.30. Mileage 36 miles total now 2312.

Oct 29, 1970 — 46th day

Paulene writing

No riding today, just walking, and that hurts a bit as our legs are not used to it. Our first job was to go and collect a couple of enormous cartons for packing our bikes in at Laredo and take them to the bus depot. After this was completed, we went to visit the Alamo. We both thoroughly enjoyed, it being such an interesting piece of the American story. I can understand better why Texans think of Texas as more or less separate from America. Afterwards we visited the Hemisphere Tower which gave us a fantastic view of the city.

The weather was perfect, and we could see to the horizon. Looks like we will have a few hills tomorrow. Right through the city are deep canals, all tree lined and very pretty.

We had lunch at an outdoor cafe next to the canal. We had tomatoes, tacos, and enchiladas. Hot and yummy, they were too. It was a really relaxing Latin sort of atmosphere. We then wandered home to the Motel and supper, TV, and writing postcards home. We should have had an early night, but we wanted to see Cassius Clay on the Tonight Show.

Oct 30, 1970 — 47th day

We left this morning at 9.30 as we didn't want to get caught up in the rush hour traffic on the expressways. Har dee Har, I think they have a late rush hour in San Antonio. That was the most unnerving time of this trip; half of the time, there was no shoulder to ride on, so we had to share the road with one hell of a lot of fast-moving trucks, cars, and buses. We were both in a state of shock by the time we got through it all. I'm sure we will look back in a few years and say, 'we must have been absolutely nuts to travel through the cities on the expressways as we did'. Now there are laws that prevent such activities.

Anyway, it was truly a fantastic day, with the sky as clear and blue as one can imagine. That is one thing we will surely remember about Texas, the clear sky.

During the day, we travelled through a few small and very western-type towns, with almost all the men looking like cowboys (most probably were too).

We stopped for lunch under a bridge so as to get some shade. While unpacking, a young guy came walking along, and after he passed us, he turned back and said where did you all come from. I told him, and he sat down as if to ponder all this, just looking at the road and conversing no more. Finally, after about 10 minutes, he got up and said see you all later and ambled off. We finished our riding day at a town called Pearsall, so we had come 55 miles. The town was predominately Mexican, as were most of the people we saw during the latter part of the day. We were lucky to get a Motel, as this is hunting season, and this is the best part of Texas for hunting Turkey, Quail, and Deer. There were some hunters there at the Motel with special four-wheel drive vehicles, behind their cars with special seats set high up from where to shoot. This seemed a bit unsporting to us, but certainly not surprising. Our total mileage now is 2367.

Oct 31, 1970 — 48th day

We did not get going early today as we only were going a short distance of 35 miles to Cotulla, the last stop before Laredo. When we packed up the bikes, some Texas hunters came over to talk and introduced themselves. Great big characters all and very friendly.

Nothing exciting during the ride today; more little western towns, great evidence of hunters, and quite a lot of traffic, most likely heading for Laredo.

Reached Cortulla at 1.00 pm and got a little cabin. Didn't think we would get one because of all the hunters, but we were lucky, I guess. We walked into town and had a look around some of the stores. Went into one Western wear store, and all around the top of the walls, there must have been 100 mule deer heads mounted. Up near the drug store, an older man was just standing outside on the sidewalk dressed in typical western wear, but he packed a revolver slung low on his hip at a jaunty angle, just like the gunfighters in the movies, complete with bullets in his belt. At first, I thought he was a Sheriff, but he carried no badge. Mileage today 35 bringing our total to 2402

Nov 1, 1970 — 49th day

Paulene writing

Well, we made it seven weeks to the day. We left Cortulla around 7.30, although we had to go back a mile to the motel as my bag was open and one of my moccasins had fallen out. Another headwind, ho-hum, but although it was 67 miles, the fact that it was the last 67 miles was a big help. We passed through a couple of small towns before stopping for lunch. A lot of cacti dotting the countryside too.

Sure wouldn't like to fall off our bikes into that. Two young brothers came to talk to us and told us about the huge ranch we were passing through. We fed the ants our crumbs and headed out again.

It was very sunny and warm, and very thirsty work. We were feeling particularly parched with only 7 miles to go when my back tire exploded, another puncture. Harry started changing the tube and tire when two customs men stopped and asked if they could help and offered water. I ran up and drained their canteen. They had big containers of water in the back of their truck too. One does not realize how good water tastes until you are without it. With everything fixed, we set off again. (on the whole trip, I had nine flat tires, and Harry had none, we figured it was because often I was riding on the inside of Harry where there were greater chances of whatever on the road that could cause a puncture).

We stopped a couple of times to take some last photos of us riding on this trip.

A very important milestone was the sign saying we had arrived at Laredo; not long after, we were stopped by a young newscaster from a local radio station. He did his interview, which was a tad nerve-racking.

We soon found a nice motel, but at $19.00 a night, a bit rich for our blood. We found a more convenient motel right downtown next door to the Greyhound Depot, and not as expensive, so everything is working out fine. Phoned Ottawa and was pleased to hear everyone is well.

Nov 2, 1970 — 50th day

Today we relaxed and tried to do some shopping in Laredo. This wasn't easy as there was a holiday in Mexico, and consequently, about a million people converged on the stores in Laredo. The quality of the merchandise was quite cheap, and we had a hard time getting what we wanted. I was able to buy a pair of Cowboy boots (still have them), but Paulene couldn't get her leather jacket. We plan on leaving tomorrow as our train leaves Nuevo Laredo at 6.30 pm.

In the evening, we both took apart our bikes; that is, we stripped off the saddlebags but threw most of the other stuff away. Also, today we phoned our bank in Canada and had them wire some more money to us.

Nov 3, 1970 — 51st day

Today I bought two packs to put our gear in. It seemed funny riding the bikes again with nothing on them. We left the Motel at about 2 pm with our packs on our backs and rode off to Mexico. (except for riding a couple of miles to the train station, we decided not to ride in Mexico on the advice of everyone from Mexicans themselves to American police) it was only about 2 miles to the border from the Motel. The customs people shunted us off to a special area, we could not speak Spanish, and they knew very little English. Finally, after about 1.5 hours of sitting and being shunted from pillar to post, we got through. We did not know, however, that they had stamped Motorcycles across our tourist cards. This was to pose quite a problem when we left Mexico.

Anyway, we were in Mexico, and what a contrast there was between Mexico and the US. It was like night and day. The poverty was unreal. It seems to us there is something drastically wrong somewhere when there is such a difference across a 50-yard-wide river.

We had a 2-mile ride to the train station, where we had a 3.5-hour wait. Most of the time, we just sat around and watched the people go by and tasted a few Mexican sweet breads, etc. When it was time to buy the tickets, there was a problem as the ticket man knew very little English and I wasn't sure what we were getting into. We checked our bikes through the cargo area and boarded at about 7.00 pm. We had a hell of a time getting to our seats because of the language situation. (one should really learn to speak the language of the country one is travelling through).

Finally, we got settled in and found our positions, and they were just as I had hoped, a lower and an upper. We were seated for about 1/2 an hour when two Mexican boys sat down opposite us. Finally, we started rolling and were underway. Not long after, a guy came through ringing a type of bell. I asked the Mexican boys if that was the dinner bell, not knowing if they spoke English or not, and they answered yes.

We got talking and found out they had just been to Sherbrooke, Quebec, in Canada for a couple of months. We hit it off very well, even though their English was not the best (certainly a lot better than our Spanish). We really got stuck in the Mexican foods and loved it. The food on the train was so cheap too. One time we both had fillet steak with all the trimmings, dessert, and all, and it only cost us $3.60 for us both.

One of the Mexican boys, Tonio, really wanted to extend some kindness to us as he had been shown that, when in Canada. When we got to the big station in Mexico City, he called his sister and told her about meeting this Canadian couple on the train, and asked if we could stay with her and her husband for a week while until our plane departed for New Zealand.

Paulene with our two Mexican friends, Tonio on the right.

She said yes and what ensued was very special indeed. Every morning for that week, Tonio would come and pick us up, and he would show us the sights of Mexico City and surrounding areas, and each night we would have dinner out with all his family. Such fun we had and learned so much about Mexican history, even the pyramids of Teotihuacan, which reached their zenith between 100 B.C. and A.D. This was so interesting to us.

So that ended this part of our trip back to New Zealand, and what an adventure it was. We flew from Mexico, had a fuel stop in Tahiti, and then on to the islands of

Fiji, where we spent a week having an amazing time travelling around the main island of Viti Levu before heading on to New Zealand, where we lived and worked for almost four years before returning to Canada.

Chapter Five

Our seven-week 820-mile canoe trip from Sault St. Marie to Ottawa, Ontario

June 1, 1974

The seed for this trip came from our bicycle trip from Ottawa to Mexico in 1970. For that trip, we wanted an adventure in going back to New Zealand for me to meet Paulene's family and perhaps stay for a while. In this case, we figured we had to have an adventure going back to Ottawa in Canada and a more settled life of work, and who knows...family maybe?

We thought, let's canoe from Sault St Marie to Ottawa. We had never done a canoe trip of any kind, let alone one that was 820 miles long. We did have camping gear, though, from our many tramping trips in the mountains of New Zealand.

We thought as well, let's go across the country from Vancouver by train to make it even more exciting as Paulene had not done that yet, and I was only six years old when I last did a cross-Canada trip by train.

The trip across was a treat for the scenery, of course, and the luxury of the train itself, from the accommodation, the observation cars, the bar car, etc., etc. We got off that train in Sudbury and took a Budd Car train from there to the Sault. We no sooner got seated and settled in when the conductor came around and, besides taking our tickets, asked us if we would like to come up front and meet the engineer. He did not have to ask us twice. They were such nice guys, and we rode up there for over 100 miles, with them telling us of life on the rails, the unavoidable accidents they sometimes had with animals, and the people they met.

They even let Paulene drive the train for a bit and do the traditional horn before a level crossing. Here is Paulene at the controls.

One always has to have their foot on the 'dead man's brake'. This is in case the engineer had a heart attack or some other event and fell off his seat. The train would come to a stop pretty quickly if such a thing happened.

We arrived at the Sault at 12 noon and, after a walk around downtown, rented a car so we could see who was selling canoes and what kinds. We also checked into the River View Motel right across from Belle View Park, where we would start paddling. We also went to the Post Office to pick up the Maps that my dad had sent to us from Ottawa care of General Delivery. Because of the length of the trip, we had to make do with 1-250,000 scale Topo maps.

Now we needed a canoe. We phoned around some of the sports shops to get ideas and opinions on various canoes based on the trip we planned. After long talks with Marvin and Bill of Currie Sports and others, we decided to try out the Grumman 15 ft. Aluminum and the Scott 15.5 ft. fiberglass models. They were both well-designed from the standpoint of stability and load-carrying capacity. It came down to a couple of points. The Grumman was noisy on the water, and it transmitted the very cold water of this area to us in the canoe, where the Scott was quieter and felt more comfortable regarding the water temperature.

We went back to the shop and picked out the one we wanted and some rope. The cost came to $214.00 with tax, a great deal as we planned on spending $350. Back to the motel and some final shopping and supper. Harry is most impressed with the quantity and quality of the young gals riding 10-speed bikes in the Sault; his eyes have been popping out.

Up early the next morning and after a quick tidy up, Harry went uptown to buy a good Silva Orienteering compass which is very accurate when using the Topo maps. It took us three trips to get all our gear from the motel across the road to Belle View Park, where we were to start paddling. Time 11 am. Here is Paulene with our loaded canoe ready to go for the 820-mile trip ahead of us, and not really knowing how long it will take, but not worrying about that either. We are starting anew in Ottawa when we get there. How exciting!

We were wondering how the canoe would manage the rather large load we packed into it, but we were soon put at ease as the canoe handled it very well. We started off in a calm which was nice. We had ideal conditions for a couple of hours, and we did 10 miles or so and stopped for lunch. After lunch, the wind picked up, and it wasn't long before we got into Lake George that the wind became a problem. As the wind was coming right up the lake, which is around 12 miles long, we were getting some rather large waves, and as we had to go to the eastern shore, we were going across the wind. Finally, the wind and waves forced us to shore as we were shipping more and more water as the waves were getting bigger and bigger and breaking into the canoe. The place where we went ashore was the Garden River First Nation Park, which was very handy. You can see Paulene busy writing up our diary. First day's mileage for 4 hours of paddling was 15 miles.

Paulene writing

We are now caught by the winds again, so we are taking a small repose on someone's cottage lawn. It is now Wednesday, June 6, and our third day of the canoe trip. After we left the First Nation's Park yesterday, we had the most fabulous time as the conditions were perfect. We set off around 7 am after a good muesli breakfast. There was a beautiful mist over the lake, and you could barely see the far shore where we were headed. The paddles dipping in the water were the only human sounds, but the birds were really going to town. My paddling contract states that every hour I can take a 5-minute break. Here I am, watching Harry paddle and watching the world go by.

We were lucky enough to catch sight of our first loon, who gave us a quick glance and then resumed his fishing. Later there were quite a lot of fishermen about, so they must know what lies under the surface. :-)

After Lake George, we were just approaching East Neebish Island when Harry spotted a beautiful white duck sitting on a log. We paddled over and saw there were a pair of them. They also spotted us and proceeded to exit, but not before we were able to get a great view of them both. No photo :-(

In the middle of Lake George, there was a colony of nesting seagulls, and boy, did they go crook at us as we got closer, even to the extent of diving as close as they could to us. I raised my paddle over my head to protect us until we got out of their space. Phew!

We found a lovely little island for lunch, and by this time, the weather was so gorgeous. The paddling was so easy and warm; we stripped down a bit and found a nice place for lunch on an Island too. Not always easy to find a great spot for lunch, but this one was not too bad. Good place to sit on the rocks and the canoe riding safely in the water below us. Paulene catching some rays on a lovely day.

The water is still too cold for swimming, especially after the waters of Hawaii. We were soon off again, enjoying a peaceful paddle, but by 2 pm, when we approached St. Joseph's Channel, the wind came up swamping strong, so we landed at a small island, hoping to set off again when the wind eased.

Harry writing

We figured that the same thing would happen as the night before, that is, when around 7 pm, the winds would die down, and you could do a couple of more hours of paddling. In this case, though, the winds did not behave as they were supposed to, and they continued on unabated. At 8:30 pm, we headed out, not really expecting to do a great mileage but mainly to find a decent place to sleep. This we found about a mile away. It was an island that had an old trailer on it, which was used for a fishing camp or something. Anyway, there was a good spot for us to pitch our tent, and we soon settled in for a good night's sleep.

This morning we awoke to a strong east wind which meant we had to paddle right into the teeth of it. So, we had a lazy breakfast and took our time packing the canoe, hoping against hope the wind would ease. It didn't. I used this time to go over the map and practice my compass and map work. Using 1:250,000 scale maps with the details so small, our bearings were amazingly accurate when combined with the Silva Compass.

Finally, around nine, we set off anyway and soon found out we should have stayed ashore. The waves were very big, and we shipped a little water. Paulene gets quite wet in conditions like this as the spray comes over the side, and she collects it. We ended up only going a mile or so and found a sheltered area and pulled up at a cottage that had not yet had its special look of peacefulness spoiled by the influx of holidaymakers.

I spoke to an older man in a cottage nearby, asking if he thought it would be OK if we came ashore here for a while. During the course of the conversation, I found out that his son had done a tour of New Zealand a year ago as an entertainer. His son's name is Gary Buck, and he is a well-known country and western singer, now in the Canadian Country Music Hall of fame.

Paulene writing

Today is Saturday, June 7, and we are in the Thessalon "Welcome Wash" washing a few clothes. Since Thursday night, when we camped on the cottage lawn, the following has occurred. First off, Mrs. Buck was terrifically kind in that she came over with some butter tarts she had baked for us with a terrific note besides. We played with a couple of chipmunks and had a nice sleep in the afternoon. After a short walk after supper went to bed early, hoping for a wind change in the morning.

No change in the morning, so we thought we would just try and get around the corner to find a better place to camp due to the poor toilet facilities on the lawn. Anyway, we finally made it around the corner, waves were high, and I got my usual soaking. We found a pretty little cove complete with a private bush, dock, and even a barbecue. Harry went and asked the owner if we could stay until the weather eased. He was a very sweet man from Cleveland. His wife was also very charming, and we had a terrific day waiting for the wind to drop.

Harry writing

For supper Friday (June 7), we had Perch, which we had caught during the afternoon. Altogether, we had six of them, very tasty if a little bony. During the cooking of our supper, the rain came down, and we must have looked at a sight standing there in front of the old outdoor stove waiting for the fish to cook. After tea, we went and paid a visit to Mr. and Mrs. Ahlering and had a terrific visit. Their cottage was 28 years old with a lot of charm. The living room was all-natural wood and had an enormous fireplace. We all sat around the fire with a Sherry and had a good old yak.

During the night, it rained and blew something awful, but with our new fly on the tent, we were completely dry and cosy. I woke up around six and looked out at the lake to see the wind coming from the SW :-). Boy, then there was some activity as we broke camp and made a big breakfast.

Saturday, June 8/74

Today was our best day so far as regards the miles covered.

Paulene writing

What wind there was dropped away completely, and we were able to make Thessalon by the evening. The day started off very misty, and we were caught in a terrific shower of rain, but the sun soon came out and dried us off. In the morning, we saw a number of abandoned cottages, mostly beautiful big old stately ones which are possibly too expensive to upgrade these days. We went and explored one, and it was simply huge. At one point, as we were coasting along between a couple of islands, Harry noticed a mouse in the canoe. He managed to put in on the end of his paddle to toss it ashore, but it fell off the paddle and, with no trouble, managed to swim to shore. Later on, I discovered where it had been in my pack as it had eaten through two blouses and made a hole in the pack, too, the little bugger.

We were lucky at Thessalon as there was a campground on the water's edge, so we were able to shower, change and tidy ourselves up before walking into town to the laundry, a restaurant, and a food store to restock. Altogether a great day.

Sunday, June 9, and the southeaster was still blowing. We left anyway and struggled to get around the Thessalon point. We ended up at a small boat dock that was so infected with bugs it had to be seen to be imagined. I was feeling cold and miserable, and Harry paddled most of the next 8 miles around lots of rocks and shoals, which afforded us some protection from the wind and waves. Finally, we reached a very exposed point and could go no further. We took shelter on the boat dock of a millionaire-type summer cottage.

Well, it then proceeded to thunder and rain harder, and we took shelter under a small verandah, thereby escaping the worst of it. We were still quite cold when it finally abated enough, and we could round the point in search of a more appropriate camp spot. One island we thought uninhabited did, in fact, have a cottage on it. We knocked on the door to be almost bowled over by an enormous English Sheepdog accompanied by three very strange looking guys, all on this little island in the middle of nowhere. They said we could camp there but also showed us where we might find something more suitable.

We set off and finally found a pretty little island covered with spring flowers and also, to our delight, two bird nests, one small one with four little blue eggs and a larger one with two large speckled eggs. After setting up our camp, we had a lovely sleep and didn't wake up until late.

Monday, June 10/74

Still a ghastly SE wind, so once again, we didn't get too far. We are camped on another small island that is quite sheltered and cosy. This gave us a chance to dry our socks and shoes over a fire.

Today is Tuesday, June 11/74, and we won't be going anywhere today as the wind and waves are too strong. Harry is fishing, and I must write to Mum.

Harry writing

Well, we ended up spending two nights on this little island as the weather was just unreal. However, we decided we would have to continue on regardless, as our food supply was dwindling fast. The bugs here were quite bad, as you can see as Paulene prepares a meal.

So, on Wednesday morning, we set off. The wind was blowing very strongly from the west SW. We had a very long point to go around just 3/4 of a mile from the island, but as this would put us out into the extremely rough waters, we decided to portage through the point. Later on, however, we still had to deal with that very rough stuff as it was the only way forward. I think I can honestly say I haven't been in freshwater that rough in any kind of boat, much less a canoe. But our little canoe is very stable, and I feel very confident with it. We still shipped a lot of sprays, and a few times, some green water would come aboard. To add to the excitement was that, along the coast, there are all kinds of rocks and shoals just under the surface of the water. If you are going into the wind, they are reasonably easy to spot as the waves would break over them. But when you are running before a strong wind with big seas, it is extremely exhilarating to be surfing along on the crest of a wave looking down, and all of a sudden, you see rocks just under the surface on both sides of you. It was an experience one won't soon forget. I wouldn't, however, like to have wind and waves like that for too many days as they are very tiring.

We got to within about 3.5 miles of Blind River when we had to head for shore again because of the extreme conditions. From our map, we saw that we could go up a little river for about 1.5 miles and then down another, which would bring us back to the North Channel, but about 1 mile closer to Blind River. While waiting at this second river mouth, we spoke to a couple of fishermen, and they showed us where we could go on a little channel used by a logging CO. This would take us up to within 1/2 mile of town. The only snag was that there were two portages.

The channel that we were in for the last 2.5 to 3 miles was inhabited by a ridiculous number of beavers. We would never have believed the destruction these little monsters could get up to had we not seen it with our own eyes; it was like Vietnam. Talk about defoliation.

Paulene getting ready to cut us a wee channel in this beaver dam so we can float through.

There were trees down everywhere, and just over from us were was another little channel, and all along, as we passed, we would hear the thump thump as the beavers slapped their tails on the water and dived to safer territory.

Monday, June 17/74

Harry writing

Well, hello again, diary.

This entry is being started at Little Current, where we are now. We had a good time in Blind River. When we arrived, there was a motel right at the water's edge, and the weather being so miserable we decided to check-in. We found out that night that we were much more comfortable sleeping in our tent than we were in a proper bed. It must be the fresh air. We had dinner at a restaurant; we both ordered a salmon steak at $3.10, but when the girl came with our supper, there staring at us were two big T-bone steaks worth $5.75. So, we had a rather nice meal for a cheaper price than it would normally cost. :-) We did all our shopping in the morning and checked out of the motel at 11 am. I even managed to get a replacement topographical map for one that I had lost just before getting into Blind River.

So, we were away again at noon with a really strong westerly blowing. It soon became apparent that we would have to stop as we were taking quite a lot of water aboard. So, we took shelter on a beach and soaked up a little sun, and read our books.

Just before coming to the beach where we took shelter, we came racing around an exposed point, riding the tops of huge waves like a surfboard, when we soon spotted a huge old steel-hulled boat that had grounded on the rocks in a sheltered area. It must have been too well-grounded to salvage it, as it looked like it had been there a few years at least.

The name was clearly visible, so I researched the boat and came up with some interesting information. Built-in 1882 for a lumber company working the east side of Georgian Bay. Over the years, it had other owners, and the information is that it was broken up in 1963. I guess breaking up just means taking all the good bits off and leaving her somewhere on the rocks. She was a handsome ship in her day that I am sure is full of memories for so many men.

In the evening with wind died away a little bit, so we could go about a mile out to an island to camp. The island was called Sanford Island. It really was quite beautiful as we had a terrific sunset with beavers and ducks swimming real close to us as we were having a coffee before hitting the sack.

Paulene writing

The next day was a very good one for canoeing, even with a slight headwind most of the day, but the sun shone bright, so we were happy. We called into Moiles Mills on John Island, but there was nobody home.

The weather turned rather foul later in the day, and eventually, we camped on Aird Island itself. This area is called the North Channel and is beautiful beyond words, a chain of islands from Blind River to Little Current. Paulene enjoying the amazing view of the North Channel islands, which we would visit again in later years.

It is now a favourite area for sailboat cruising, and we have been back on short canoe trips specifically to enjoy the amazing scenery and Islands. We camped on Aird Island, we had a thunderstorm at night, but no worries to us as the new fly on the tent works great. Because of the storm, we did not get away too early the next day. We crossed to Crooks Island, and it was foggy and chilly.

We followed down Eagle Island to the Benjamins, encountering rather high waves en route. The Benjamins were fabulous as it was the first time we had seen the pink rounded rocks shaped by glaciers, no doubt, which we have found more of in this neck of the woods. We camped there overnight and left once again in a dense fog. It was calm, though, and we made good time and photographed one of a few lighthouses protecting these rocky shoal-strewn shores.

We passed many other islands and eventually arrived at Little Current and camped at a campground of sorts about a mile from town. In the morning, we paddled to the town dock and were thrilled to see all the services available right by the water.

Did laundry and were most surprised to meet up with one of the women we had met on the cross-country train, "The Canadian". Also talked with some Sailors and some other young people and enjoyed this little touch of civilization again before we paddled on our way again, but we didn't get too far because of the high waves. We sheltered all afternoon on a boat dock of an abandoned house.

Getting ready to head out again. Paulene waved at the Seagulls. Conditions calm, so we will take advantage and get some miles in. Sometimes on Georgian Bay, the wind will come up strong after lunch and force us ashore.

Later on, made it to another island for the night and woke to a downpour, so Harry spent his birthday in bed until 11 am eating peanut butter sandwiches and liquorice for breakfast.

After the rain stopped, there were 2 hours of hard paddling around a big point. Any big point of land or the point of an island have to be handled with care as the waves sometimes increase going around or the waves bounce back at you and cause a more difficult situation than the large waves alone. After passing along many beautiful islands, we portaged on a voyageur portage. This is always fun as you imagine yourself walking in the footsteps of history. Here is Harry in the canoe at the start of the portage.

The Portage was from Frazer Bay to Killarney Bay across the Badgeley Point. Then we hit windy Killarney.

Killarney presented an attractive mix of old docks, buildings, and a fabulous old shop where we did buy a few more goodies, even butter tarts. Leaving Killarney on the narrow channel, it is situated on then, rounding the point where we stopped for a few hours in the sun washing our clothes and ourselves too. Lovely pools of warm water formed in these beautiful Canadian shield rocks that abound in the area.

When the wind died down, we paddled off across the first part of Georgian Bay and how beautiful it was. We camped on a rocky island (they all are), but Harry found a nice soft bed of moss for the tent. After a relaxing meal, we felt like our old selves after all the rough conditions we had experienced previously.

Harry writing

Off again in the morning at about 10 am in very nice conditions, the sun was out, and the sea was calm. We went about 6 miles, and then a wind came from the SW came up, and briefly, we experienced the largest waves of the trip so far. They were just too large, however, and we had to wait for things to quieten down as we had to go around a rather exposed point.

Paulene writing

We had high waves and southerly winds, and a thunderstorm. Saw a sailboat moored in a dangerous position possible right off an exposed point of land, which is just asking for trouble. We made camp near Pt. Grondine, which just lies west of the western channel where the French River pours into Georgian Bay.

Friday, June 21/74

We left early and had a very good day, sunny and strong northerly winds. After passing the main entrance to the French River, we came across a deserted fish factory complex and spent a couple of hours looking at fabulous old buildings and the bones of an old open fishing boat.

This old steam warping tug or Alligator boat was among the items left behind when this plant was shut down or mothballed. I'm hoping to get a more definitive purpose for this piece of equipment in this particular place. This is a very basic version of Allitgator boats that could winch themselves overland between lakes to collect logs and drag them back to bigger water.

The area is famous for its fishing. We stopped in at Key Harbour for supplies and talked to a young family holidaying there. Key Harbour is completely serviced by water. The railway used to come down here but no longer does.

In the afternoon, we had and strange experience as we saw a young guy stranded on a lonely, small rocky island with no tent or anything to protect him. He did not even have any matches, so we gave him some of ours. We found out later that these boys are left in these remote places for seven days. They are from reform schools, and I guess it's supposed to make them think and appreciate life a bit more. The young couple at the wharf had found one of them crying, so not knowing about the reform school thing, they had rescued him and taken him to the highway to hitchhike home. We made camp in another thunderstorm with lots of bugs.

Saturday, June 22/74

Our greatest day yet, around 30 miles. The wind blew hard from the north, so we almost surfed along. The Islands out from Bayfield were beautiful, and we came across the entrance Pointe au Baril which has an old lighthouse, and there must have been some fishing industries here at some stage as there are many abandoned buildings. The Ojibway islands were a very attractive area that we passed during this great day.

Sunday, June 23/74

Got going around 10 am and spent a terrific day in the sunshine being pushed along by a light northerly wind. We stopped at Snug Harbour for supplies.

You can see why this is called Snug Harbour, well sheltered from the big waters of Georgian Bay itself.

The island we camped on now is so beautiful, and we are situated on a great beige-brown rock with our own bay and an island directly out front. The water so calm and pinkish as the sun sets behind us. The mosquitoes are happy with our company in the evening too. We saw two minks swimming in front of us, one having a mouse in its mouth, perhaps taking it back to hungry young mouths. We have seen lots of mother ducks with their broods, some as many as 12.

Monday, June 24/74

Last night was funny because we were raided by a hungry Raccoon. First off, we heard him rattling around under the canoe, which wasn't too bad as the food was in the tent with us. Guess what? It wasn't long before he could smell it inside with us and tried to find a way in. Harry set up a store of ammo to throw at him, but each time Harry would get back in the tent after throwing things at him, he would come right back for another go. Harry remembered reading in one of Farley Mowatt's books of staking out a territory around his tent with his own pee, and the wolves respected that territory and would not cross it. Harry did this around our tent, and coincidence or not; we did not have any further trouble with Mr. Raccoon.

We stopped at San Sousi Marina. Harry called his parents to let them know where we were and how we were getting along. We also saw that Samuel de Champlain had been to San Sousi before us. There are a couple of plaques commemorating their passing this way in 1615 and 1685. How neat is that?

We had a terrific long day, around 30 miles, and did not stop until around 9 pm. The mozzies were waiting for us again. We were also dive-bombed by some Sea Gulls when they decided we were too close to their territory.

Tuesday, June 25/74

Set off around 10 am, bright and sunny, with a NE wind gently helping us on our way. We were lucky enough to get really close to a Common Merganser and her chicks; the camera was not accessible, so no photos. Not many boats around at this time, and we hope to get to Honey Harbour around noon. Not much was happening at Honey Harbour except millions of moored boats, but we had a good walk around. For camping, we were directed to Beausoleil Island National Park, not far away. We got caught in a couple of thundershowers on the way, but no problems.

The facilities at the park were great, and we both enjoyed a hot shower, our first in a couple of weeks. Harry lit the fire in the camp stove, and we had a yummy supper, dry and sitting up at a table. In the evening, we had an enjoyable time sitting around the campfire with a nice couple from Orangeville and their 15-year-old son. They warned us of the Raccoons, but we got away with no trouble during the night.

Wednesday, June 26/74

We woke at about 8 am to a calm sunny day and left around 10:30 after a big breakfast. We were both much refreshed after our touch of civilization. We hope to find a supermarket and coin wash at Port Severn later today.

This was also going to be our first lock on the Trent Severn system, which would take us to Trenton, Ontario, on the Bay of Quinte. We found out that if we registered our canoe and got numbers for each side of the bow, we could be locked through all the locks in the system. This worked well for us as we were on a seven-week trip and loaded with gear, which would make regular portages anything but simple. This first lock (for us), #44 was unique in that it is a railway lock.

This shows Paulene in the canoe at the dock of the Big Chute railway lift lock (#44). In 1976, it was finally decided that a new, enlarged railway lift would be built. The current carriage was opened to the public in 1978 and can carry a boat up to 100 feet (30.48 m) long, and 24 feet (7.32 m) beam. It cost $3 million to build. The older one that we used is shown here. An interesting thing about Parks Canada and the operation of any of its locks is that there is a rule regarding canoes is that they had to run you through the system or help you portage around it. We were heavily loaded for our long trip, so an actual portage would have been a pain for us ourselves or for them to help. The older railway lift is still in place but not used. You can see the new larger railway lock in this photo.

The lock master was great, and no trouble for him to lock us through even though we were the only ones at the time.

After shopping, we had lunch and a beer with a couple in a houseboat moored next to the canoe. We were lucky to be there as there was a violent thunderstorm at the time. We camped overnight at the Marine Railway and were very impressed with the facilities at the lock, and it was the same at all those locks where you can stay the night.

Thursday, June 27/74

Left at 10 am on a fantastic sunny warm morning. The lakes we are going through are like glass. We are actually travelling upstream now, and the current does seem to slow us a bit. The two fellows who we talked to at the locks came up in their boat to see if we would like a ride and a tow but naturally declined. We had lunch at Swift Rapids locks with a friendly old dog, but the flies drove us away. We stopped at 6 pm at Lauderdale Marine, which is at the South end of Sparrow Lae, and lucky for us, they had a coin wash, a rather run-down campground, though.

Lock 43 is isolated with a sense of wilderness and, therefore, not practical to drive to by road. This is the deepest single-chambered lock on the Waterway. An impressive area makes a quiet stop for boater camping and picnicking for the self-contained boater. It is a pack-in, pack-out station. Paulene looking gorgeous as we wait to leave the lock.

Friday, June 28/74

Got going late today as it was just hard to get into gear. After coming through lock 42, we were hailed by our friends in the houseboat; we stopped at the next marina and had a beer with them. Sharron and Capt. Bluebeard? Later we came across a little bit of bad weather towards the end of our crossing at Lake Couchiching, but the majority of the crossing was OK. We found the Provincial Park at Mara point, which was completely full and turning people away as this is now the July 1 weekend. Luckily for us, they let us camp on the beach.

Saturday, June 29/74

Woke up in the rain, but luckily there was a covered shelter near the tent so we could pack up out of the rain. We left to cross the upper part of Lake Simcoe at 9:45, and so far (halfway), it is smooth as glass, with light rain falling.

Harry writing

Well, the rest of the crossing was reasonably uneventful except for the rain, which kept up for the crossing, but we could not complain as the wind was light. At the first lock we went through, we were put in with five large Chris Craft Cruisers as well as two smaller runabouts.

All people were friendly, and we would have been tipsy had we accepted all the beer that was offered to us. We managed to keep up with these folk as we went through 5 locks together. We stopped and camped at lock #37 and again met some very friendly people. Before we set up camp, we paddled down to a Marina, hoping to get a few groceries. Paulene had just got out of the canoe when a middle-aged couple came up and started to talk. They were very friendly, and he had been to New Zealand a number of times as he sailed with the Port Line. Paulene found there were no groceries at the Marina, so our newfound friends offered to drive Paulene to a store a few miles away, and that's how we finally got our supplies. Later on, as we were sitting by our tent having a coffee, another couple came by and even offered a room at their cottage for the night.

Sunday, June 30/74

We got an early start today as they were predicting rain, and at 6:30 am, it wasn't raining yet, so we decamped, had breakfast, and were away by 7:30. The wind was strong, but fortunately, it was almost on our backs. We had quite a rough crossing of Balsam Lake as there were thunderstorms all around. We arrived at the town of Rosedale on the east side of the lake and thought we would look for a motel as it is our 7th anniversary today. As I was trying to find the owner of the motel, the cruisers we had gone through the locks with the day before, as well as our friends on the houseboat, came through, so there was much waving and hollering. The women who managed the motel, even though they did not have any vacancies, offered to put us up for the night in the old office. But she was determined to find us good accommodation and phoned all the motels in the area, and finally, through the Chamber of Commerce in Fenelon Falls, we located a room at a Motel in Fenelon Falls.

An old shot showing the lower wharf and locks that get boat traffic around the falls

So, off we paddled to Fenelon Falls, about 3 miles across Cameron Lake. It was a very rough crossing, and we shipped quite a lot of water. Who did we see as we arrived but our Houseboat friends Stu and Sharon. We called the Motel owner, and he came to the water's edge and picked us up with a lot of our gear. As Stu and Sharon were to be here for a couple of days, we were able to leave our canoe on top of their boat and a lot of our gear also.

Paulene writing

As this was our wedding anniversary, we didn't want to cook our own supper, but the only place we could find was Sims Grill. The fish and chips were fine, so we enjoyed the meal. We called in to let Stu and Sharon know where the motel was, as they wanted to call and take a shower.

Monday, July 1

Lovely fine day; Stu & Sharon arrived at about ten, so we had coffee at the Motel restaurant while they showered. We sure had some good discussions with Stu, who seems rather intelligent and quite vocal in putting his thoughts across. We sunbathed and rested until late afternoon when we walked down to the shops to buy a few things; then, at 7 pm, we went to the houseboat for supper. There was another couple invited also. Wendy and Dave, two school teachers from Toronto. We had a fabulous meal of barbecued steak, salad, bread, wine, and strawberries. We felt a bit wobbly as we went back to the motel around 11.

Tuesday, July 2

Woke up early and arrived at the houseboat to collect our canoe and stow our gear for the following day. Finally said goodbye at about 9:30. After passing through the lock, we stopped on the other side and picked up some groceries. Very windy and wet trip through Sparrow Lake, especially the first half; we were shipping a lot of water. Finally arrived at Bobcaygeon at about 5 pm, where we camped at the locks.

Bobcaygeon is a neat holiday-type town (in summer), and we went for a nice walk and coffee in the evening. Harry painted the name Walkabout on the stern sides of our canoe. This comes from our first adventure together in Australia, which we called Walkabout, a word referring to the Aboriginals of that country that often just took off into the country on an apparent whim, and the term given to that behavior was Walkabout.

That night the heavens opened up, and never before have we heard such loud thunder or brilliant lightning. It was really incredible, the ground almost shaking. I doubt there was one person in Bobcaygeon that slept through that one.

Wednesday, July 3

We woke to a windy, humid day, so we decided to stay there for the day. Spent most of the day reading and doing a little fishing below the dam. Took a walk in the town during the afternoon; all in all, a very relaxing day.

Thursday, July 4

Left good and early and crossed Pigeon Lake with little effort in good conditions. After leaving Buckhorn, a fantastic storm came up, and some cottagers hailed us as we paddled by, inviting us to shelter with them until the storm abated. When we settled in with them, they mentioned a form covered over on a couch at the edge of the room. The lady said it was her mom who went through the Blitz in London during WW11, petrified when big storms like this one hit nearby.

The storm ended, and we continued on our way. It was a long day, and we finally camped at the locks at Burleigh Falls. This is a very attractive part of Ontario, as are most of the lakes in the Kawartha Lakes region.

Friday, July 5

Made a very good time today going down Clear Lake, through Youngs Point, down Katchewanooka Lake, Passed Lakefield locks #26, and saw our old friends on "MyTwo Cyns", whom we first met at Lake Simcoe. Then on down to Peterborough and its famous lift locks, which have been here 70 years. It has been designated a historic site as well. We had the whole campground to ourselves, and the view was beautiful, the trees so green with rolling hills behind.

Saturday, July 6

What a beautiful day, absolutely perfect for a little paddle. We left the Lift Locks around nine and had a leisurely breakfast. After a mile or so, we came to Lock 20 on Little Lake. We crossed the bay to buy some groceries, then came back and camped at lock 20. After lunch, we went for a walk-in downtown Peterborough and also went to a political meeting for Pierre Trudeau, which had an exciting atmosphere. Two days later, the Liberals would secure a majority Government. Finished the day with a nice meal and a leisurely evening.

Sunday, July 7

Left early with good weather and next camped at the Serpent Mounds park, Rice Lake. The exhibition of the early Native Mounds was very interesting, and we felt lucky to have been able to see it.

Had a nice talk with a French fellow from Toronto who was also a canoeist. We had a hard day paddling before reaching Rice Lake as most of the boaters were Sunday boaties, as we called them, and showed little respect for us, hardly ever slowing down, so consequently, the waves they created were a problem.

Monday, July 8

Election day today, and we were so pleased we had attended the Liberal Rally for Hugh Faulkner in Peterborough, as it made us feel somewhat involved. The weather today is very hot and humid, so perhaps we will get a thunderstorm soon. We had a pretty long day as we were heading for Campbellford. As usual, the Lockmaster there was happy for us to camp at the locks, so while I went shopping, Harry painted 'Walkabout' on the other side of our canoe. In the late afternoon, Harry went to mail my postcards to New Zealand and also to call his family in Ottawa to let them know of our progress. Well, what great news he had on returning to our camp. Apparently, his old boss at the museum had phoned his mom, telling her that there was a vacancy in the photo section if he was interested. Yippeee!

(I have to explain the above call from my old boss. Gerry and the crew at the photo section were sitting around at lunch playing cribbage and listening to the local Talk Show host on local radio. The subject was something like 'How come, young people, were not as involved in travels to other countries as previous generations were?' Harry's mom was also listening and decided to phone into the program, telling the host of her son and wife on this long canoe trip back to Ottawa after living in NZ for a few years. She did not mention our names, but Gerry knew the caller's name was Foster, so he figured this must be Harry and Paulene returning from NZ. Gerry called every Foster in the phone book until he reached Harry's mom and gave her the message for Harry to call ASAP.)

Tuesday, July 9

Woke at 5:30, so we were on the water by 7:30. We saw some Carp mating in the reeds and were able to get quite close to all the jumping, splashing, etc. These non-native fish seem to be taking over territory from other species like Bass, Pike, etc. Mostly on quiet rivers today, so I had the radio going, and it was good company, as quiet river travel can be a tad boring because it's so easy. Arrived at the Trenton Locks and set up camp. We told the lock master about leaving our canoe, tent, and gear while we made a quick bus trip to Ottawa. He said no problem and would watch over our gear.

I called my old boss at the museum, and he told me that the fellow who took my position on our going to NZ had left, and he had to fill that position fast, so could I come back ASAP for an interview? We went to Ottawa by bus on the 11th and did the interview on the 12th. When he told me I had the job and asked how soon I could start. I told him we needed two weeks to finish the canoe trip. He was shaking his head, said oh, okay. What followed was some quick visits to family nearby and then back to Trenton Saturday morning, and everything was intact.

Sunday, July 14

Left early, very hot weather, around 90 degrees F. At one point we stopped and had a swim at noon off an abandoned dock.

The paddling was quite good, just a few rough patches. Around 6:30 or so, as we paddled along the south shore of the Bay of Quinte, an elderly gentleman with a long beard hailed us from the shore, asking if we were looking for a place to camp. He invited us to where his dock was and said to put our tent up on the lawn behind the cottage and then come in for a drink. Behind Paulene and our canoe at the dock was

Angus's pride and Joy, a historic boat that he lovingly restored over a number of years.

We did as we were told, and on entering, he introduced himself as Angus Mowat and introduced us to one Barbara Mowat and another lady whose name I forgot. As we were chatting and enjoying a drink, I could not help but notice photos on the walls by John de Visser. I knew John de Visser to be a friend of Farley Mowat, so I shyly asked if Angus was Farley's dad. He was. Farley was one of our favorite Canadian authors. My one VERY real regret was not photographing Angus, me being too respectful and not wanting to intrude on his space. He was so interesting and has had such an incredible life, much like Farley. We have since read and thoroughly enjoyed the books that he has authored.

Monday, July 15

Very rough, windy weather, but we made it to the start of Long Reach, where the weather was much better with the wind behind. Stopped in a cozy little possie for lunch and finally reached a provincial park where we camped. It was called

Adolphstown. The park was steeped in early Loyalist history, and on the property is The old Hay Bay Church, dating from 1792. We had a lovely walk in the evening and stayed up chatting with other campers near us.

Tuesday, July 16

Got on the water at 7:30 and had a favorable wind. We had hoped to go further but found a great place to camp near the water. It was called Fairfield Historical Park and was another treasure from the Loyalist days. Featured at the park was an old house built by the Loyalists in 1793. It's great the way the different parks are centered around something of historical interest. This park had road access, so there were lots of big posh trailers, RVs, and loud people. Had a walk in the evening, a swing in a park, and Harry climbed an old elm tree.

Wednesday, July 17

Away early and took no time getting to Kingston, surrounded at times with large fantastic-looking sailboats. We also canoed below the walls of the famous Kingston Penitentiary, constructed in 1833.

We started up the Kingston to Ottawa Canal system and went to the Kingston Mills locks, only to be told we could not camp there. Made it to the next set of locks (Lower Brewers) only to be told we could not use the washrooms. Quite a different start on this canal system compared to the Trent Severn system.

Thursday, July 18, 1974 (our son John would be born this day in 1983)

Slept in this morning. The weather was cloudy and likely to rain. The scenery in these lakes (Whitefish) was very attractive and easy to see why they were so popular. Very pleasant day on the water, canoeing very close to a Blue Heron at one stage. We reached Chaffey's Locks later in the afternoon and camped on the point overlooking Lake Opinicon. Went to the Opinicon Lodge for a delicious and wholesome meal.

(Side note here Harry and his family would come here when Harry was only nine years old, and it was a favorite spot for his dad, who loved bass fishing. Harry remembers the water in the locks being as clear as glass right to the bottom, and when he and his brothers would fish in the locks, they could manoeuver their baits to the fish they wanted to catch, 10ft down in the water. Water is not as clear now but still respectable.)

Friday, July 19

This was a long hard day as the winds were from the north, and we shipped some good splashes over the front (Paulene gets those). Caught in a terrific thunderstorm on the Big Rideau Lake, too, wet and a tad cold. We camped at a marina on this lake and had a hot shower which refreshed us no end.

Saturday, July 20

We got a good early start, thanks to some rowdy kids from New Jersey who woke us up. :-) Another long day against a northerly wind. Went through Smiths Falls, another old town on the Rideau Canal. It also features a historic railway swing bridge and a railway museum.

Finally arrived at Merrickville, which had a lively group of people in various cruisers moored there. Merrickville is an interesting old town full of grand and historic buildings. A very popular tourist destination for Ottawa day trippers.

Sunday, July 21

Left Merrickville with the first lockage at 9:30 am as we were headed for Burritts Rapids to rendezvous with the foster family for a picnic at the locks. We arrived at noon and were thrilled to see our nephews Robbie and Stephen from Montreal, as well as Mom and Dad and brother Tom, with his partner Jo Ann. We enjoyed a lovely picnic and a delicious summer punch to go with it. We lazed about the grass, talking and laughing until around 4:30 when the family headed back to Ottawa, and we set off for Kemptville park for the night. It turned out to be the most disappointing and unattractive campsite of the trip.

Monday, July 22

Left Kemptville at 9:30, and it was going to be a hot day. We had a stop at Black Rapids, quite close to Ottawa. This is an attractive park setting that is popular for picnics and fishing.

It was a long day of approx. 29 miles, and as it was the last, we were keen to get to the finish line at the National Arts Center and start our new life in Ottawa.

The trip was seven weeks, and 820 miles and the seed were sown for many future holiday canoe trips following the historic Voyageur canoe routes.

Chapter Six

Lake Superior North Shore by canoe, Cloud Bay to Marathon August 1980

Seeing there is only Paulene and me, plus our canoe and gear, we have to figure out how to arrange to get our stuff at the starting point and the car at the finishing point. The other option is to leave the car at the start and find a way to return, and get it from the finishing point. For this trip, we took all our stuff west of Thunder Bay to where we would start in Cloud Bay. We met a nice couple there who had a cottage on the water, and they kindly agreed that we could leave our canoe and packs with them until we had taken the car back around to Marathon and then found our way back to our gear and canoe.

We left the car with the police in Marathon for safekeeping in their lot. We then hitchhiked back around to where we left all our stuff and the start of our paddle. Phew!

June 29, 1980

We are off on our latest leg of Superior, leaving from Cloud Bay along the coast and into Crystal Bay a bit before heading over to Victoria Island. We coasted along the north shore and passed Jarvis Island, which once had a mine on it.

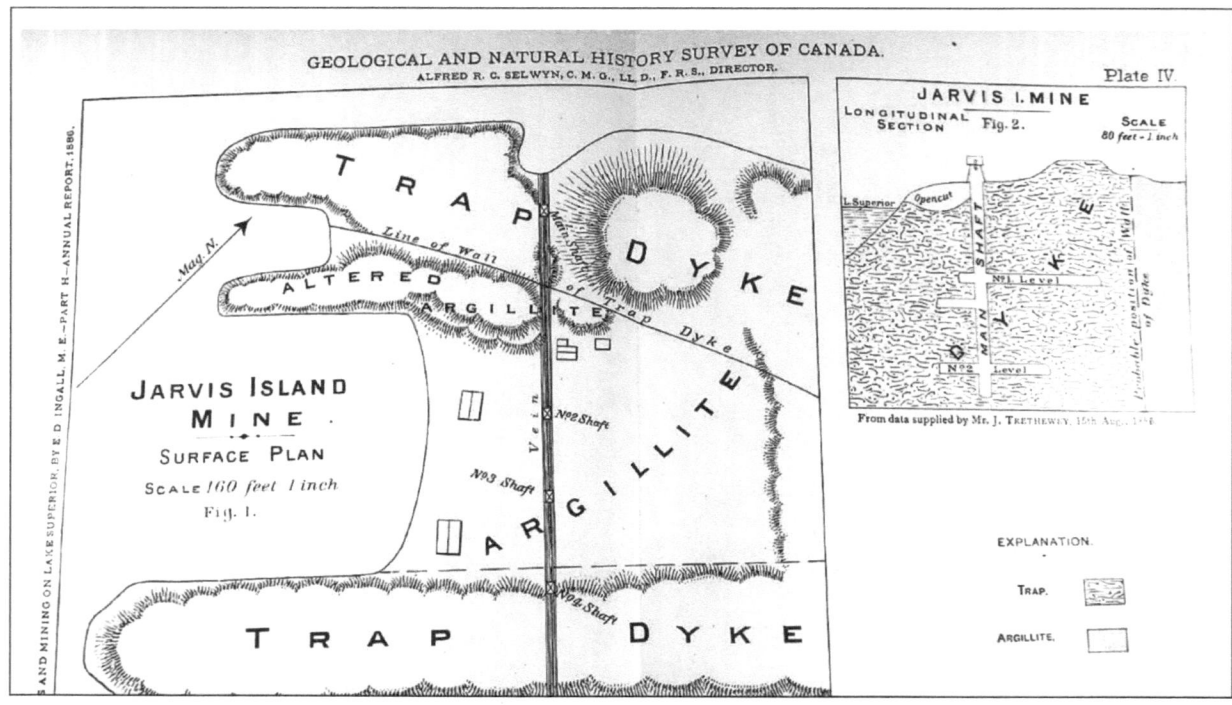

We then paddled over a short channel to Spar Island, it too had a mine, and we could see some of the traces.

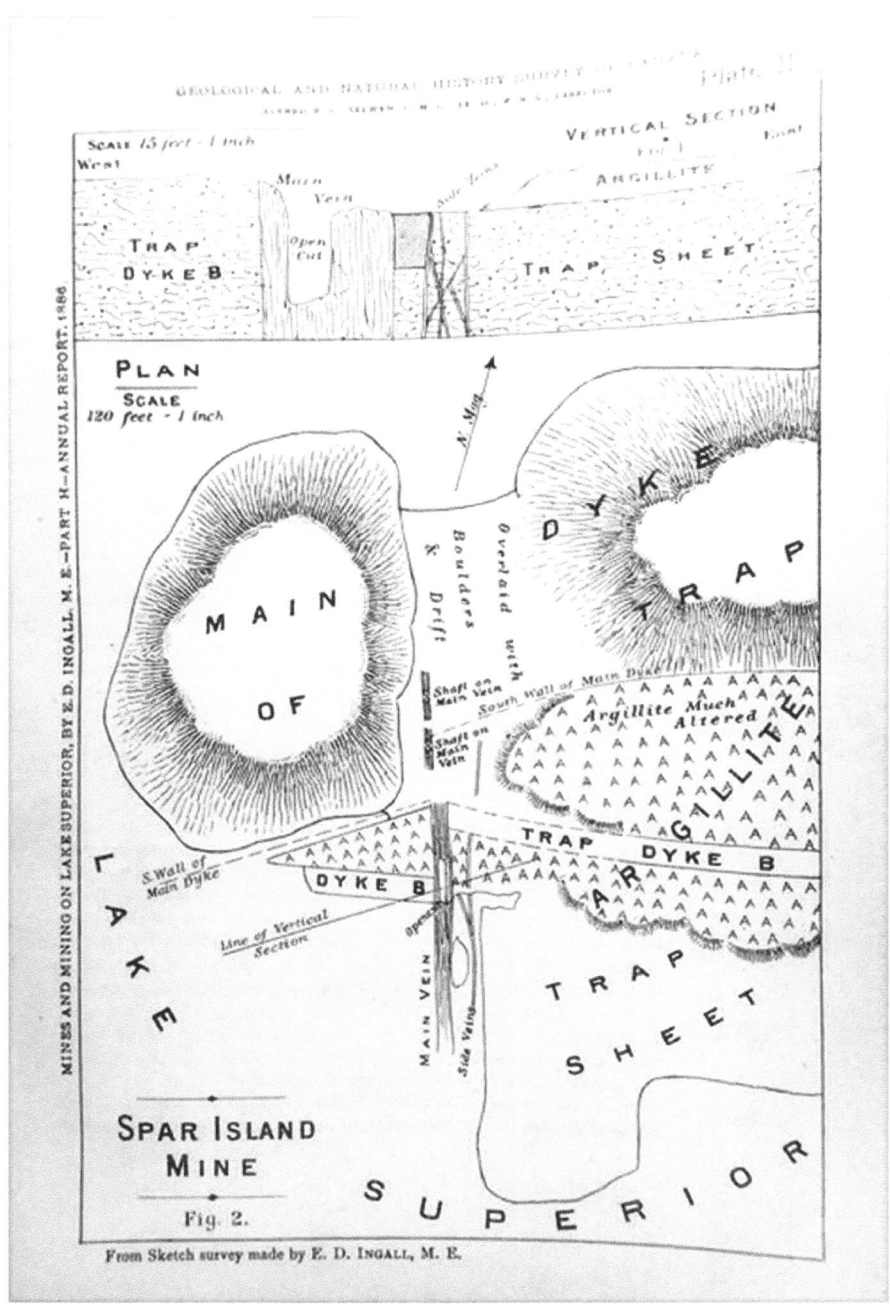

Spar island is quite high and would provide a great view from the top. We carried on passing Slipper Island on the south side and then went up the west side of Thompson Island and camped on Anderson Island just off the end of Thompson. This was our Camp #1, June 30, 1980, and our anniversary too. This shot shows Paulene looking up at where our tent was to be, and this shot shows Paulene shows she decided to lie in the sun for a while before doing the climb up there. We had a great view from here, and this a photo showing Paulene in a dream state as she looks over the water.

People were also looking up at who was looking down on them from this little island.

We got a good start next morning, but the wind soon came up, so we took shelter on South McKeller Island, where we waited most of the day before we made the crossing to Greenstone point on Pie island. Of course, there was a mine here in the day as well. These map images give an exact image of the construction, depth, and other features. Thanks to the Geological and Natural History Survey of Canada.

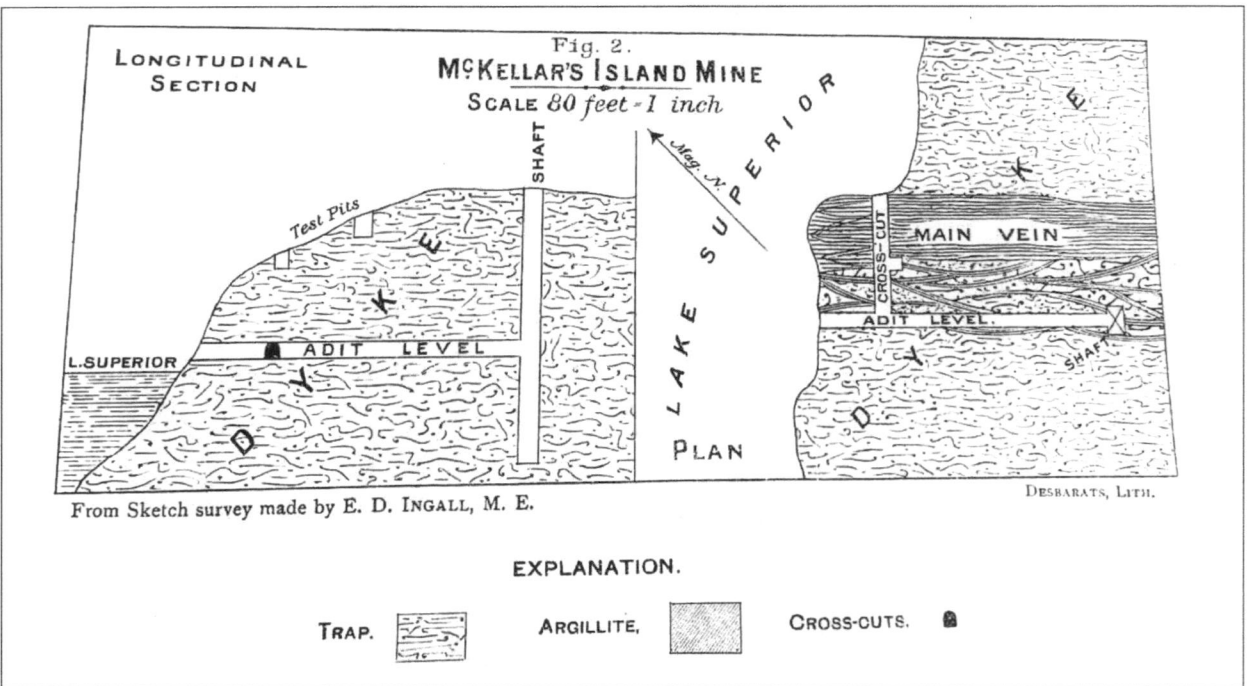

Besides the mine on our island, we soon found out there was a Blue Heron nest not far above our heads in the trees on top of the island what a racket was made when an adult came in with some food. One has to hear it to believe it. Here is a shot I managed to get of one chick, the other mostly hidden. There were also Herring Gull chicks very well camouflaged here and there, so one had to be careful walking about.

We paddled on to Turtle Head at the end of Pie Island, where we sat in the canoe and ate our supper before crossing the main channel to Thunder Bay and to the Sleeping Giant. We waited in the middle for a bit so a large freighter could go ahead of us.

We went right ashore and set up a camp as it was getting late. As I was preparing this image, I noticed for the first time what looks like a small shack in the middle, a couple of inches from the right side of the photo. I guess we did not see it either when we arrived or when we left in the morning, or I surely would have taken a photo of it.

July 2, 1980

We had a good day today, covering approx. 34 km and going through a mix of big water and narrow channels between Islands. Here is a shot taken on one such channel, showing a field of daisies.

We often went ashore when coming on a scene like this to have a look, enjoy the flowers and stretch our legs.

Almost everywhere we stepped ashore, we would see signs of moose. I just wish we had seen a live one. Another neat scene we came across when going ashore for a break is what I think is Cushion moss.

We also saw an amazing display of rocks, I think, known as organ pipes. The first time we have ever seen this.

I think the following explanation describes this Organ Pipe Rock formation. These 2.5 to 2.8 million-year-old **basalt** lavas, commonly known as trap rock, fractured during cooling into vertically standing, hexagonal **basalt** columns. So much to see and wonder about as we paddled to our Camp 3.

Such fun when we can explore a quiet shoreline in some of these channels, not always having to pay attention to wind, waves, and obstructions just under the surface.

During a break, this shows how our canoe looked as we paddled along. Everything covered and protected against a sudden rainstorm or rough water.

July 3, 1980

39km today, a mix of islands and bigger water, crossing near Gourdeau Island and then through a channel between Spain and Bordon Island. Then along the southern shore of Lasher Island, then over to Coutlee Island, then to the tip of Brodeau Island, where we went ashore for a break. Then across to the north end of Spar Island (there are 2 Spar Islands) where we made our camp 4. There is some history of an old mine here, but details are scarce.

The black sand here is magnetite that was ground out of the region's bedrock by glaciers during the last ice age and by tens of thousands of years of weathering and water-mediated erosion. The black sands found along the beaches of Lake Superior contain trace amounts of placer gold. The occurrence of this gold has been known for a long time, but in general, it has gotten very little attention because of its small size and difficulty to mine.

Paulene helping to unload the canoe ready to set up our camp. Looks a tad messy, but underway everything is under wraps and tied in.

July 4, 1980

40 km today. Starting off and headed to Fluor Island and through a narrow channel, which we always loved exploring, and even stopping so Paulene could wash her hair.

This narrow channel, like others, showed pathways made by moose as they crossed from one side of the channel to the other. I wish I had photographed one or two, as they were like moose highways. We then passed between Fluor and the small island called Tisdal Island.

We stopped at the tip of St. Ignace Island for lunch. The English name is a translation of the original French name given to it by Jesuit missionaries in honor of their founder St. Ignatius of Loyola. The island is clearly depicted on the 1669 map "Lac Tracy ou Superieur avec les dependances de la Mission du Saint-Esprit," attributed to Claude-Jean Allouez and Jacques Marquette. We carried on up the shore of this large island, then between it and Bowman Island. The maps now show a lodge called Bowman Island Lodge where we passed…that was not there in 1980 when we did our trip.

On we continued passing through a narrow channel between St. Ignatius Island and Armour Island, where a 20th century nation called Republic of Nirivia was formed. On we went, eventually stopping to camp on a small island off the eastern tip of St. Ignatius Island.

July 5, 1980

Short-ish day today at around 24 km, ending at our camp 6 site on Cobinosh Island, south of the larger Wilson Island. We started by heading across a bay to the end of Bead Island before turning towards the westernmost part of Simpson Island. We paddled along the shore, enjoying the sights as always and thankful that there is very little to none in the way of man's stamp on this beautiful wild, and rugged shore. We came across a great beach where one could find Amethyst and other rocks of interest. We also find along the shores of the lake a diversity of wildflowers as well as lichens and mosses.

Snuggled away in a cosy spot with flowers

It was not long before we left Simpson Island in our wake and headed across a bay to work along the shore of Battle Island. Battle Island has a lighthouse on the western end that was first established in 1877; it also had a copper mine or exploration site at one time. We often found native copper just below the surface of the water. You never know what you will see next.

It was not long before we reached Cobinosh Island, where we set up camp and were windbound until noon the next day.

July 6, 1980

33 km today, taking us a few km east of Terrace Bay to a lovely quiet spot for our camp 7.

Paulene getting ready to use the new stove we just built. Happy days.

Paulene getting comfortable in her new kitchen. What a view.

First, after leaving Cobinish Island and at Barr Island, we headed across to Copper Island, then over to Les Petits Erits, where we stopped for lunch. A couple of kilometers later, we crossed a big bay to Blain Island, then across another bay to a point around which is the Terrace Bay Nature Reserve and a large beach which is the start of some hiking trails.

Our feeling of a very remote canoe trip has temporarily changed as there is some civilization on our left. A few kilometres more, and we are on our own again and at a lovely secluded beach for our camp 7. Here are a couple of shots of my gorgeous wife Paulene, one cooking and one just looking gorgeous. What a mate she has been, going on for 54 years.

Paulene just made another stove and has the billy and some grub on.

Here just looking gorgeous.

July 7. 1980

Left our lovely spot and headed out, even though the winds were quite strong. We could feel the end of this trip not too far away and wanted to get some mileage done today. We crossed Victoria Bay and the swell and winds from the south kept getting stronger as we rounded the point. All the while one travels along the Superior shore; visual treats appear in the form of different rock formations that stick out from the norm.

Down into the bay, we went, and around St. Patrick Island and over to a beach where we went ashore to have a break from the conditions. Whenever we were on shore, we enjoyed the wildflowers we would find in the most amazing places. You just can't stop nature from showing her face, no matter the conditions.

Back on the water in an hour or two, but only got 4km before we landed on an island called Lawson Island. We stayed here as the wind was just too much.

This was an interesting stop as there was an abandoned cottage that looked like it had been built as a hippy haven, with walls of books and mirrors everywhere, including on the ceiling over the bed. Also, on the high point of the island was a marijuana grow-op that had been all busted up. Our theory was the Island was raided. I was sure I had taken photos (even B/W's) of this place but couldn't put my hand on them, and not being with the slides of this trip. Only 14 km today due to conditions. Here is Paulene getting our kitchen set up, sawing a bit of wood, etc., 14 km today.

July 8, 1980

We got away early on this home stretch heading around a large point and then turning north, following the shoreline as the large bay was too far across for the conditions. Prairie River Mouth Provincial Nature reserve on our left. Then heading southerly as the shoreline went. We went around a point of land between us and Pic Island, made famous by the group of seven artist Lawren Harris. What a beautiful painting, and to think we paddled between Pic and the mainland.

We stopped for lunch and a rest here before pushing on to Marathon.

On our way again and after a short distance, we went on the inside of Foster Island (no relation, darn), then on to Detention Island. Neys Provincial Park, of which Fosters Island is a part. During World War II, 35,046 prisoners of war and Japanese Canadians were held in 26 main camps in Canada. The north shore of Lake Superior was the site of three such camps: Neys, Angler, and Red Rock. Neys Camp interned 100 mostly German POWs and some Japanese-Canadians between 1941-1946.

Paulene resting and no doubt thinking of this leg of the North Shore, which is soon to end, and how much we will miss this incredible place.

After Detention Island, it was a straight line to our landing spot at Marathon. I soon walked up to the police station and retrieved our car. We did 47 km on this last day. This leg of Lake Superior in 1980 was the last of 3 that we did of the North Shore. These trips have been life-changing as, without a doubt, these shores are magical; the secrets they hold and the beauty they show us is beyond imagining.

Chapter Seven

Lake Superior North Shore, Marathon to Michipicoten August 1976

Aug 1, 1976

This was actually the first leg of the North Shore that we did (which was the middle of the 3) from Marathon to Sault Ste. Marie in 1976. The photo here is what we found after leaving Marathon and going around the point of land that provides a sheltered bay for the town. We paddled right into it in order to get this photo. The paper mill was the big employer at that time and according to a good friend who worked in that industry for years, says company philosophy relating to operations in the hinterland like this was "The Solution to Pollution was Dilution".

The North Shore of Superior was, and still is, relatively untouched with the clearest, coldest water you can imagine. Thank goodness that what we see in the photo above no longer exists. The mill went bankrupt in 2009, and the site was demolished and cleaned up. No decision as to its future use yet. See, mankind can learn from its mistakes, but I don't think we are yet winning the war with pollution, and it's not dilution.

As it was 5 pm when we started, and we knew we would not travel far before finding a camp for the night. Turns out we just did approx. 10km before stopping in a protected little bay. This photo shows how beautiful it was and another shows the far end of the beach with logs scattered around.

The beach where we came ashore to make our first camp was so well protected, at the bottom of a bay. Our first taste of wild Superior, very little signs of other people having been here before us, logs that escaped the fate of going through the mill, and lovely peace and quiet… except for the waves.

We got going again in the morning, and we were soon going around the first of many large points (Randle Point) of land that we had to be careful with. This being a very rocky shore, when the waves hit a rocky point, they bounce back off the rocks and create a more dangerous situation than the waves alone. We often had to give the point a large berth, so we were beyond the point of the waves bouncing back, causing us any problems. We then crossed Heron Bay, almost 1.6km across. If you wanted to cross one of these bays, you had to know the conditions were not going to change for the worse while doing it.

After crossing the bay, we paddled into an area called Prospect Cove. Close by on the shore, there is a hiking route that features places where members of the Group of Seven Painted. These trips are put on Blaq Bear Eco Adventures and other tour operators.

We continued around the shore and through a narrow passage between Channel Island and the mainland and soon to where the Pic River empties into Superior. There was an old trading post located here, and just upstream, a little over 3km, there is the

Pic River Indian Reserve. This is also where the Pukaskwa National Park starts and continues south to just past the Pukaskwa River.

We did not travel too far before going into a little protected cove where the headquarters for the Pukaskwa National Park headquarters are now situated. When we were there in 1976, the Park had not been formed yet, and the land behind where we camped was just wilderness. We ended up spending three nights at that campsite as the wind was too strong on the lake. We hiked around behind our beach and even portaged our canoe to a body of water behind us, taking fishing gear, etc. As you can see, I caught a nice Pike that we took back to our camp for dinner that night. Paulene on the way back to our camp, coming through some wildflowers.

Aug 5, 1976

Finally, the winds died down on the lake, and we were off again, rounding Campbell point and ongoing between Picture Island and the mainland, us watching Otters as they watched us.

Otters are a common site on the North Shore if you keep your eyes open.

What a glorious day it was as we paddled on, exploring and enjoying the views as the day progressed.

Paulene enjoying her 10-minute break (in her contract ;-) each hour, taking in the views and thinking how lucky we are to be here.

Going past Morrison Island, Sewel Point, Gids Harbour, and soon crossing the big mouth of Oiseau Bay. There are hiking trails established now around parts of the coast of Puckaskwa National Park, with official campsites along the way. There was none of this in 1976 when we made our trip. This coast was as it must have been for hundreds or thousands of years. Now when one looks at Google photos from the area, lots of these hikers build cairns or Inukshuks with the round Lake Superior rocks. This is a shame and inconsiderate for those who would love to see this amazing coast as it was for millennia. Here is a shot of Paulene and our canoe after we landed near our camp three spot and a photo of this log-choked river as we walked up a way. We covered 39km on this lovely day.

Aug 6, 1976

An easy and short day today, just covering 18km; as always, though, very interesting picking our route with a compass and map in amongst islands and bays. In lots of areas of this coast, there are views that show just how rugged and potentially dangerous life can be in a canoe unless you take all the precautions with lots of common sense.

We stopped at the point where the Swallow River empties into Superior. We found a trappers' cabin, and here is a shot Paulene, sitting in front of it. She proudly showed off a blood donor tee shirt. (She was director of the Ottawa Red Cross blood donor clinic at the time).

The cabin was not far from the shore; we soon saw it was open and even had some food inside to provide someone help if needed. We did not need the food but slept there that night. I realize now, all these years later, that this was a small part of an important history and community of trappers in this part of the country. We paddled up the Swallow River a piece to the picturesque falls that lie there.

Aug 7, 1976

This was a pretty easy day of paddling of 27km until our camp 5. We passed the historic Otter Island with a lighthouse on the western end that was established in 1903. We did touch the eastern end of the island before crossing to Otter's head and passing near Deep Harbour. Pointe Canadienne was a big point to go around and one that would need a lot of care and caution in windy weather. We were lucky as the wind and waves were calm.

There are so many of these glacier-created scenes as you paddle along Lake Superior's shore.

We crossed the last bay before rounding another point to where we would stop for the day. We arrived at this lovely beach about a half mile from the Pukaskwa River. We made camp and, in a short time, realized we would be there for more than one night.

Paulene had an early-term miscarriage; she was not sure she was even pregnant but knew the signs of a miscarriage as this was her 5th. We knew what to do and the position she should be in to prevent or reduce any bleeding. I noticed some fishermen out on the bay, so paddled out to speak to them. They said they were camping in the area and would ferry us to Michipicoten if necessary. We also had three great sunsets at this place that will always be remembered.

Paulene's next pregnancy (1982) would end in our miracle baby boy, who has grown up to be a newer and improved version of me, according to Paulene.

Aug 9, 1976

The paddle from Camp 5 to 6 was only 14km long with respect to Paulene's miscarriage. We set up our camp on a small island, and we got a lovely moonrise shot towards Michipicoten Island.

Aug 10, 1976

24 km to camp seven on a great day, passing Ganley Harbour, which is the entrance to the Ganley Harbour Provincial Wilderness Area and a haven for sailors looking for a secure and safe harbour. Later on, we paddled through Le Petit Mort Rocks; not sure how they got this name, but very interesting scenery nonetheless. We stopped to have a warm lunch and dry out at a sheltered little cove and later stopped at Cairn Point.

Before making this trip, we consulted with Eric Morse who mentioned this cairn and that most travellers stopped here and added a rock to the cairn. We met

Eric and his wife when we travelled up the Ottawa Valley on our way to a canoe trip, and pulling into a gas station at Cobden saw this car with a canoe on top. I spoke to the occupants, who turned out to be Eric and his wife. From then on, when doing our 3 Lake Superior trips, we consulted with Eric before heading out, and he would pass on interesting things to look for and give us an idea of what we would face as he and his wife had done the whole north shore too. I have not been able to find a photo of the Cairn as it is today.

We carried on and found a lovely beach where we could set up our camp

7. Paulene seen here taking in the amazing view and peace of our very own beach.

Aug 11, 1976

Headed out on a good day, soon rounding Point Isador. We were then faced with 8 km of cliffs and very few places we could get to shore if we had to. The wind and seas were okay, so we headed out, sure we could get past this area. Three plus km after rounding the point, though, we thought we should look for a place we could go ashore until things calmed down a bit. Headed in, and just before hitting the shore, I jumped out, hoping to ease the canoe ashore rather than crashing it onto the rocks.

Just then, a wave grabbed the canoe and turned it broadside with me on the shoreside. I was afraid the next wave would hit the canoe and knock me down. I managed to turn the canoe a bit and get it on shore. This was the closest we had ever been to dumping a canoe.

We stayed for a couple of hours until conditions got better, and we could carry on. One always has to have an eye on the weather, especially in an open canoe. This shot shows how cold the water is and the lighter colour in places that give you a good idea there might be trouble under the surface.

This photo shows just how wild the winter storms can get, preventing much from growing near the water's edge as the waves will crash ashore and wash any soil off the rocks, not giving anything a chance to grow. 21 km today from camp 7 to camp 8.

Aug 12, 1976

This was the last day of this leg of the North Shore that we were to do, and it was a day of dense fog. We just paddled on by compass and map as one could only see a few metres. This was a little stressful at times, but I had long ago learned not to go against the compass bearings. We did stop and take a photo of us both and our trusty

Scott canoe, as it just seemed the right thing to do. As you see, we relied on heavy woolen sweaters to keep us warm, even when damp or wet. We finished at Bucks Marina (not sure of the name in 1976), which was the starting point for our 1979 trip from Michipicoten to the Sault. Approx 32 km on the last day of this leg.

Chapter Eight

Lake Superior North Shore, Michipicoten to Sault St Marie, July 1979

As mentioned before, when it is just us making a trip like this, we have to figure out a way to take our gear to the start place and, ideally, have the car at the end point of the trip. For this one, we found some kind folk at a marina at Michipicoten that would look after our gear while we took our car back to Sault St Marie, where we would finish. We were lucky, and we left the car safe and sound in the police station's secure lot in Sault St Marie.

Then, off to the Bus station only to find the next bus heading up the North Shore was already full. I asked the driver if he would mind if we sat on the floor in the aisle between the seats, as we really did not want to spend the night waiting for another bus. So, that's what we did, chatting to people above us on either side. Oh, to be young again!

Jul 15, 1979

We got let off on the Trans-Canada highway at the road that would take us down to Michipicoten, canoe, and gear. It was good to get loaded up and on the water, making a start on this latest trip. We no sooner paddled out of the Michipicoten river onto the lake when we realized the wind was too strong and the waves too big to try and make many miles. We landed on a very large beach and came ashore to get our bearings.

We went down to the end of the beach to set up our camp. Only 4km today.

We tucked our camp down at the end of the beach, where it was more protected and private. You can see our canoe tucked in the corner.

Jul 16, 1979

On the water early this morning to get some miles in, so we skipped breakfast until we reached a lovely protected harbour called Brulé Harbour

We paddled in here for our breakfast stop. Very happy to have done 16km so far today. Paulene whipped up our breakfast so we could get going again on this lovely day.

The harbour was named after this famous European Explorer who was the first to journey beyond the St. Lawrence River into what is now known as Canada.

Off again after breakfast, and in a few km, we would round the huge Cape Chatillon. One has to be very cautious rounding these big capes, especially in an open canoe. On the NW side of the cape are steep cliffs rising right out of the water, and these waves bounce right back out, and dealing with those bounce-back waves, as well as the ones coming in, can create a dangerous situation. Sometimes it is best to go further offshore, where you don't get the effect of the waves bouncing back. There is a Canadian Coast Guard rescue boat named Cape Chatillon, in fact.

Not long after rounding the cape, the wind came up again, so we looked for a place to camp for the night and found one right ahead on a lovely long beach. Another 18km under our belts today for a total of 34km.

Jul 17, 1979

We got away early as the day looked perfect for some serious paddling. Cape Gargantua was 8 km or so away, and lots of nice scenery getting there. As you look at these steep rockbound shores around Lake Superior, you notice there are no trees growing close to the shore. That's because when the storms come and huge waves crash on the shore, they wash all the soil from the cracks in the rocks and give nothing a chance to grow.

The top photo on the next page shows what Lake Superior looks like in a winter storm when the waves hit a large cape. Photo credit Duluth News Tribune.

On rounding the cape, we came to Devil's Chair, which was an interesting island, mostly rock, with a hole one could see through.

We stopped for breakfast on Dixon Island, about 4km east of the Devil's Chair. Then continued on exploring into Gargantua Harbour and beyond; always so much to see and wonder about as we progressed. We stopped for breakfast on Dixon Island, then down the coast we went stopping where Baldhead River empties into the lake.

We explored that for a bit, Paulene looking to see if any fish were in the pond below the falls. We can just imagine how much water comes down this river in the spring judging by all the logs strewn around on higher ground.

We continue on our way and, in a few km, stop and have a look into Robertson Cove. Love the glacier-shaped and formed rocks one finds all around the Superior Coast.

These glacier-formed rocks are so beautiful, and in the sunshine, when warm, they are so nice to lie on and soak up that lovely heat.

We continued on and, after a total of 39 km, camped on a lovely Island that reminded us of our typical camp spots on Georgian Bay. Tent on rocks, held down by rocks, no fuss, no muss.

What better living room could you ask for and a view over the historic Lake Superior.

Jul 18/1979

Now back to the trip. We headed out, soon passing Sinclair Island and Sinclair Cove. The cove is a well-protected harbour that is popular with the cruising set. Then we paddled on to where the Agawa Rock Paintings are; this one is the most famous of those I photographed.

The ultimate source of the Agawa Rock site as it exists today is Thor Conway. His book Spirits on Stone (the 2010 edition of a book first published in 1991) presents the pictographs in the voice of the descendants of the Ojibwe who painted them. Conway identifies 117 separate pictographs at the site and provides the most informed commentary.

After the amazing visit to this site, we paddled on in a bit of a dream state with lots to think about regarding the rock paintings, their origin, when done, etc., etc. As I look at Google earth today and see how much development there has been since our trip in 1979, there were no official campsites, few trails, just a wild, and free wilderness. We passed Agawa Bay and around the coast, and just before Montreal River Harbour, we stopped for lunch at a beach. Montreal River has a number of power generating stations on it before it discharges into Lake Superior.

We continue on past the Montreal River Provincial Park and the new addition to the Lake Superior Provincial Park and around the mighty Theano Point to a beach that afforded us a nice place to camp and views back to the point, which was another subject of the Group of Seven artist Lawren Harris. Paulene looking happy in her new kitchen. What a spot, what a view of this historic lake that has seen so much history take place.

Jul 19, 1979

Up and away early on what looks like a great day for paddling. It was not long before we were rounding a large point of land called Pointe aux Mines. In November 1849, a force of Anishinaabeg and Métis warriors, forced the Quebec and Lake Superior Mining Association to stop operating at Pointe aux Mines, Mica Bay, Lake Superior. As always, when canoeing around the shores of Lake Superior, you are treated to some amazing islands and scenes of rocky shores to cement memories that will last a lifetime.

After ten more kilometers and a stop for lunch, we arrived at modern-day Mamainse Harbour. 6,000 years ago, Indigenous people started mining copper in the Cape Mamainse area. Today, there is still local mining exploration at the New Mamainse Harbour 7 km north of the older harbour. As we entered the channel leading to the harbour, we came on one of the old-style fishing tugs. This one was called the James D.

Besides an interesting history it was actually the only boat that would go out and search for the Edmond Fitzgerald when it was caught in that storm in November 1975. Gordon Lightfoot wrote the definitive song about that tragedy.

The next 18km around the coast before reaching the spot just past Pancake Bay Provincial Park, where we would have our Camp #5. As we can see, the end is a couple of days away. Paulene said let's take a couple of photos of us at this time. This was a good day of 40km and lots of memories.

Jul 20, 1979

Off at a good time this morning and a little nervous about some big crossings we had to do, so hoping for some good weather. The first was Batchawana Bay, fully 5.5km across a lot of open water. No sooner had we done that when we had to cross the southern entrance to this huge bay. That was another 5km across. We had a pretty good idea of the weather ahead of us at any time as we carried a dedicated weather radio with us. We stopped for a break on rounding Rudderhead's point. We then cut right across Bluewater Bay (not a very deep bay but following the actual shore would have increased the mileage a fair amount), then about 3km after crossing Sand Bay, we made our camp for the day and were glad to get those big crossings today behind us. The shoreline today was not the typical rugged Lake Superior shore we have come to love, but more built up and populated now that we are getting closer to the Soo.

Jul 21, 1979

In just over 4km, we had to cross another large bay, this one called Goulais Bay, which was 6km across. The wind came up some, and so we decided to camp not long after doing the crossing, having only gone 14 km in total. We were pretty sure we could make the Saul tomorrow as the weather looked promising, and we had just had approximately 34 km to go.

Jul 22, 1979

Got a good start today as we started to round the large Gros Cap and further on reached Gros Cap Bluffs. For those travelling east to west, it must have been a sight to behold after coming so many miles in relatively protected waters from Montreal or even points east and now faced with what looked like an ocean ahead.

We carried on around past Chene Island and then Pointe des Chenes Park, around Pointe aux Pins itself. Because of the number of tall red and white pine which grew there and its physical location, it was a natural and logical area to start a shipbuilding industry. This took place on the east shore of the cove at Pointe aux Pins. We carried on crossing Leigh Bay, then rounded Old Vessel Point to, where we went ashore on the property of the Algoma Steel works.

Two security guards came along in their truck. This was very advantageous to us as they very kindly helped us lift the fully loaded canoe into their truck and drive us to their gatehouse; then, one officer drove me to the city police station, where we had our car safely parked in their lot. A fine end to a great day and another inspiring canoe adventure.

Chapter Nine

Our fifth French River Long Weekend trip, June 1980

From French River Supply Post, down the main channel into Georgian Bay and back up the Key River.

This is a favourite long weekend trip of ours on this historic river. We have done this five times now, introducing friends and family to this amazing river that has seen so much history. This time it is with work colleagues and friends Jean-Pierre Hardy, Nicole Casteran, Terry and Nancy Ruddell. Jean-Pierre and Terry were both historians with the Museum of Man in Ottawa; Nancy also worked there as an educator. What better people to share such a trip on this famous old highway of the past.

The French River was used as a transportation corridor by the Algonquian peoples of this region. The Ojibwa named it Wemitigoj-Sibi. It became known to Europeans as the "French River" because it became associated with French explorers of the 17th century, including Étienne Brûlé, Samuel de Champlain and Pierre-Esprit Radisson, and missionaries.

Other explorers who later followed this route included Simon Fraser, Alexander Mackenzie and David Thompson. Here is a map of these long weekend trips, starting at top right.

We leave Ottawa very early on these trips and drive to the French River Supply post, where we launch and start the trip in the late morning. The first picture shows what the area looked like as Paulene and I waited for the others to push off from the dock and what it looks like now. What a difference 40 years make.

New photo by Steve Carey

We are off, heading down the French River; the bridge in the background is Highway 69. Jean Pierre and Nicole on the left, taking in the scenery that only gets better as we go.

The first small portage is around the Recollet Falls, named after the Recollet Fathers, who were the first to use the French River, the most direct waterway to the west. The Recollet Falls is the only major drop along this section. The wooden drag way that one could drag a canoe around the falls on all the trips we did, does not appear to be there any longer, perhaps removed when the area was named a provincial park. The first photo shows the team in the process of portaging around the falls and getting ready to bring the canoes using that wooden drag way I mentioned. Our friend Jean Pierre in the foreground even looks like I imagined the French Voyageurs to look like.

The voyageurs would doff their red caps and murmur a prayer before the crosses erected here at the Recollet Falls- as many as 30 on one bank, according to a traveller here in 1800. Even today, the Falls still drown the unwary, so be particularly careful, especially in high water, in approaching the portage on the south bank very close to the top of the falls. There are Indian pictographs on the canyon wall above the falls. The above information from the book 'Canoe routes of the voyageurs by Eric Morse, First published in 1962.

The gang enjoying lunch overlooking the falls with much talk about the famous people that passed by this very place. Just look at that view and all that wondered what was around the next bend. What an amazing view looking west down the river. After lunch we head down river to our first campsite.

You can see the excitement on Nicole's face and Jean Pierre looking confident

Nothing too difficult about this kind of water; just keep the bow pointing downstream.

We arrived at the island where we usually have our first camp, Canal Island, situated at a point of the French River where you can choose a number of ways to go down to Georgian Bay.

Setting up this tent is a community affair, with Jean-Pierre standing back watching the action, and then he and Nicole go off to a cosy spot and put up their tent.

Then the kitchen has to be organized and food prepared for some hungry paddlers. After that, a nice evening sitting around the fire and then having a good night's sleep.

Everyone was up early, raring to go the next morning. I took a couple of shots of this lovely spot before leaving, one of a view from our site looking west towards the Western Channel and the other of some glacier and weather-formed rocks.

After our tents have been taken down, some discussion takes place here, probably about how we are going to get all that gear neatly back into the canoes.

The next photo shows Jean-Pierre and Nicole paddling down the Main Channel towards our portage point around the Dalles Rapids. The distance was approx. 7.5 km, and at one point called 'The Elbow', you had to know which way the channel was; you had planned on going down.

The portage was only about 200 metres long through the bush and over rocks etc. At one point, I took a partial shot of the rapids through the trees.

I think most people use the portage as we did, but I guess those with a lot of experience running larger rapids might run these. This next shot is at the end of the portage showing the three canoes and loading taking place. One might ask why three Scott Canoes. Ours is the one in the foreground, which we loaned to Jean-Pierre and Nicole. Paulene and I borrowed my sister and her husband's canoe, seen at the top. Paulene and I found the Scott to be well-designed for its carrying capacity while still maintaining a good freeboard and the confidence it gave us in large waves on bigger water.

On the channel below the rapids, only a few traces remain of the village of French River, developed briefly on the site that was to be Coponaning. The site has been named as one of Ontario's Ghost Towns and is located just below Dalles Falls. Once home to over a thousand people during the summer months at the peak of the logging days, now abandoned and dismantled, but evidence of the town still remains. The site can only be accessed by canoe or kayak. An old mill foundation just north of the existing lighthouse remains to show that this country was not always wilderness. Along the water's edge, several old boilers rust away. Also, the remains of perhaps an old fishing vessel burned to the waterline; the old boilers were too heavy and difficult to remove after the mills were dismantled

But of the two mills that worked here in the 1890s, the houses for 300 people, the two hotels and the matching churches, Roman Catholic and Anglican, very little remains. Most of the buildings were torn down and shipped to Toronto for reassembly in the 1930s; almost all of the others gradually fell victim to fire and rot.

Still, it is a place of romance and legends, a place where you can picture the barges being loaded in "the Creek", the shingle mill whining away in the Loading Cove, the rotted roads created from wood slabs and sawdust in a land where no gravel was to be found. The frontier once more delayed, the promise of settlement once more defeated, the mouth of the French now reverts back to the alders, sand cherry and pine of the wild. Information in the two preceding paragraphs from the book *'Canoe routes of the voyageurs'* by Eric Morse, First published in 1962, and Wikipedia.

Now we are getting out of the river and into the amazing islands (see map) and how easy it might be to get turned around from where you want to go. Everyone was happy to be out of the confines of the river and out into the open and endless views of Georgian Bay.

We reach our second campsite after 17.5 km winding through the islands. Here I am, busy getting the fire going after unpacking the canoes.

Later Terry reads us a bit of history he brought along for just such an occasion as we sat around the fire.

In the morning, Terry thought to take a photo of Paulene and I as we were just getting ready to head out to our final campsite.

At the same time, this rather large water snake came out of hiding to wish us a bon voyage. I'm glad we saw this on land rather than in the water while swimming!

Speaking of snakes, this is the 5th time we have done this trip and have never seen a Massasauga rattlesnake. Reading accounts of canoeing the French in recent years, a lot of people have seen these snakes...up close and personal too.

Look at the map image at the start of this episode and see just how many islands there are to explore and navigate through. A familiar scene is the Jack Pine trees bent over from the prevailing winds on a lot of the islands, made famous by the Group of Seven and others.

It was not too hard of a paddle to where we were going to set up our 3rd camp, which would give us easy access to the Key River in case the weather the following morning might prevent us from finishing in time to drive back home later in the day. Here we see Nicole giving it all with a good stroke while JP is following her lead, and later the two canoes rafting together for a break.

We arrived at the island that we have camped on four other times; such a perfect sheltered spot it is too.

The second shot shows Paulene modelling a survival Jacket we would use on the last leg of our canoeing on the north shore of Lake Superior later in the summer. The water so cold in Superior that one would not last long if you were upset and were kilometres from shore, as is often the case as you cross big bays. This jacket would give you approx 4.5 hours to get out of trouble.

After setting up the tents and getting our dinner cooking, there was time for a wee libation and chat around the fire. My dear Paulene, lost in thought while I was taking this photo.

Nothing like a good sunset through the Jack Pines of Georgian Bay to promote a sound sleep.

A rainy start to our last day on the water, but all were still smiling, happy and looking forward to starting the day

It did not last for long, though, and we had a nice paddle up the Key River. The Key river entrance from Georgian Bay looks nothing like it did in 1980 when we did this trip, let alone in the past. A good shot of Nancy and Terry Ruddell looking good in this incredible landscape as they paddle up the Key River.

Here is a funny shot taken during a break on the Key River. Terry had slipped on some algae-covered rocks and had fallen into the water when getting out of the canoe, so he put on a pair of Nancy's pants that were handy. Here he is striking a pose for the camera...and posterity.

Paulene leading the way up the Key River on our final leg. A favourite view of Paulene, as on all our many trips, she leads the way and usually gets the wettest when waves slop over the sides. Also, when we are in big following waves and sometimes surfing on them, she sits a long way from the water. Never afraid and always confident, what a girl.

Another great long weekend canoe trip comes to an end, and which is the end of this book which pays tribute to my dear Paulene and some of the adventures we shared together.

Our greatest adventure though was having our son John after 5 miscarriages. Paulene loved kids so much and always hoped we could have a family. The photo below is my all-time favourite of her and John.

In 1987 I had to photograph the Fireworks being let off from behind the Parliament buildings in Ottawa with the Museum of Civilization in Hull, Quebec in the foreground. The place I chose to do this was from the roof of a Hotel near the Museum. Paulene and John came with me, and Paulene brought a mat they could sit on as I was going to be there for a while. Note the rope that is connecting her to John. Always a good idea when on a tall rooftop with no railings.

So, Paulene lay on the mat, and John got on her tummy. I'm not sure what was so funny, but to me, it is beyond priceless. Having John was the best and most long-sought-after adventure we ever had.

Lastly, a poem I wrote to Pauline back in the '70s:

Paulene

When we first met in the world down under

our hearts were two and far apart

but strangers we are no longer

Our hearts are one and ne'er to part

Together we have tramped this earth

in lands both far and near

and sailed upon her mighty seas

knowing happiness, sorrow and also fear.

Always there to turn and talk to

she is the light that often guides me

always there to sing and laugh with

she is the fuel that always fires me.

Of mountains of hills and rolling plains

her home was where the Kiwi reigns

from this land of beauty seen

comes my wife, her name's Paulene

Epilogue

Since those stories, we had a dream in 1980 to find a property on the north side of the Ottawa River where we could build a smallish passive solar house that would be easy to maintain so we could continue to visit Paulene's family in New Zealand.

We moved in during 1982 and have been living our dream ever since. While we were building, we lived in a small trailer on site, when Paulene got pregnant again. We went back to her doctors in Ottawa and they said all was normal, but not to fret about it, just get on with your life. Miracles of miracles, John was born in July of 1983. Paulene wanted to be a stay at home Mom and she did that, creating a great environment for not only John, but some of the neighbour kids as well.

When John went to school, Paulene volunteered there, and it was not long before they hired her, she having such a special connection with kids, and worked in this field until she retired.

She developed breast cancer and after 12 years it metastasized. She passed on this past June 2022, leaving a big hole in my life and everyone who knew her.